Separation Anxiety
Versus
Containment Phobia

Why Is Your Dog Destructive When You're Gone?

Also by Karyn Garvin

Dogs Do Go to Heaven!

&

How to Walk Your Dog on a Loose Leash:
The Integrated Approach

Separation Anxiety
Versus
Containment Phobia

Why Is Your Dog Destructive
When You're Gone?

Karyn Garvin

**Divine
Dog
Books**

Also available as an eBook
www.DestructiveDogs.com

Divine Dog Books
Divine Dog Books
Tucson, AZ
DivineDogBooks.com

DISCLAIMER AND/OR LEGAL NOTICES:
The information presented herein represents the view of the author as of the date of publication. The lesson guide is for informational purposes only. While every attempt has been made to verify the information provided in this report, neither the author nor her affiliates/partners assume any responsibility for errors, inaccuracies or omissions.

Publisher's Cataloging-in-Publication data
Garvin, Karyn.

Separation Anxiety Versus Containment Phobia

Why Is Your Dog Destructive When You're Gone? / by Karyn Garvin

ISBN 978-0-984 4613-4-9

1. Dogs – Training.   2. Dogs – Behavior.

I. Garvin, Karyn, 1953   II. Title

SF431.G37 2015   636.708   2015911785

Book Editors: Bridget Magee www.BridgetMagee.com
Carol Calkins Productions

Cover Artist & Illustrations: Frankie Cadillac at 99 Designs

This book is dedicated to … **The Dog**

The Dog

is God's way

of showing unconditional love

in a form we won't reject.

Contents

About the Author

Karyn Garvin

The "Divine Dog" Trainer

All dog trainers teach through stories. Karyn's stories just happen to be based on her belief in the "Divine," that power which is greater than ourselves. Her integrated approach to dog training includes spirituality, psychology, etiology, science and the natural order of life as we know it.

There are only a handful of people who have been training dogs professionally for as long as Karyn has. "Professionally" is the key word here. This has been her livelihood, working at it full time since 1977. She was a professional dog trainer before it was really even known as, or considered, the popular profession that it is today. Certainly she has also ridden the tides of change that have affected the dog training industry from then until now.

Karyn has always loved working with dog owners and coaching people as much as she loves training dogs. She favors working with people and their dogs on an individual basis first, then furthering their training by enrolling them in a group class when they are ready. The advantage group class training has after the completion of individual training is that it allows each team to polish their skills in a distracting environment. Conservatively, at this time, Karyn has given no less than 40,000 private lessons where she has taught dog owners how to train their dogs.

As a young child, Karyn moved with her family from Iowa to India. In India she was deeply affected as she experienced the harsh realities and living conditions of that country. She was left with a burning desire to help others, and to make a difference in the world. Those experiences, along with her college studies in behavior modification, have also contributed to making Karyn the trainer she is today.

Much of what drives Karyn is her commitment to saving pets' lives. Too many dogs and cats are relinquished because of behavioral issues that were not dealt with effectively by their owners. Karyn has discovered numerous opportunities to be instrumental in the field of dog training through her own inventive solutions. A key way in which she measures her own success is by identifying needs and filling them.

She found just such an opportunity on September 4, 1993. She was called to a client's home to help with a thirteen-year-old male poodle that had been marking in the house his entire life. What Karyn discovered was that all of the traditional methods of managing a male dog that marks would not work here. This dog had Containment Phobia, which meant that restricting his area to a crate or a small room had even more grave consequences for the owner. The wife had given up on trying years ago, but it was her new husband who came up with the idea of calling a dog trainer.

Karyn remembers the very moment that the new solution came to her. She was sitting at the customer's kitchen table and asking the universe, "God, what am I supposed to tell these people?" It was then that the idea flashed into her mind. In order to continue giving the dog the freedom to move around the house, he would need to be diapered. This thirteen-year-old poodle quickly changed his troubling behavior after peeing in his diaper only three times.

Karyn went on to create the first professionally retailed diaper for male dogs, the MarkOut® Wrap, and wrote the training manual, MarkOut® Marking. She promoted the new product and method of training over the internet: **www.MarkOut.com.** Today, diapering a dog is a well-known method in the dog training world.

When pot-bellied pigs were all the rage in the 1990s, Karyn was inventive in running the world's first pot-bellied pig obedience class. She was there to help those pet owners learn how to live harmoniously with their new pets. You can still view the documentary video by going to her website **www.GarvinsDivineDogTraining.com**.

In 1998 she expanded her dog training business to include the Invisible Fence® Brand solution, and became a dealer for Southern Arizona. As she grew familiar with the standard training procedure for Invisible Fence® Brand dealers, she found a need for a better way of training. Once she had developed, tried and tested her new method of training dogs and cats, she shared it through the Invisible Fence® Brand network. They adopted the new method of training now known as the Perfect Start™ Method that is used by dealers across the United States. She was also fundamental in authoring the original Perfect Start™ training manual.

Soon after opening her Invisible Fence® Brand dealership she discovered another need. As a dealer,

Karyn found that her business was servicing more "Houdini" dogs than she had ever encountered as a dog trainer. Owners, looking for solutions to keep their escape artists from breaking out of crates as well as jumping fences, often contact a pet containment business like the Invisible Fence® Brand for solutions. While a pet containment system can be part of the solution, dealers and dog owners still need to understand the condition thoroughly in order to manage the behavior.

It was then that Karyn first coined the term "Containment Phobia" and created the distinction between Containment Phobia and Separation Anxiety. Her article was first published in the Invisible Fence® Brand Dog's Life newsletter in 2003. It was later published in the *International Association for Canine Professionals' Safe Hands Journal* and was an important advancement in the treatment for Containment Phobic dogs.

At present, her passion is centered around sharing what she has learned over her long career by means of books, webinars and speaking engagements to usher in The Integrated Approach as a method of training to the dog training industry.

Karyn currently lives in Tucson, Arizona. For the growing list of books she has authored and websites she has developed, you can always stay up to date by visiting **www.KarynGarvin.com.**

Introduction

The purpose of this book is to save dogs' lives. I've often said that dog training has a lot in common with rescue groups in that we save lives too. The difference is that dog trainers have the distinct advantage and privilege of being able to save dogs before they become homeless. Still to this day, the majority of dogs that end up being killed in shelters were released by their owners because of behavioral issues the owners did not know how to manage.

When a dog's owner doesn't understand why the dog is destructive, or what to do about it, they suffer and their dogs suffer, too. It breaks my heart when I think of the number of homes that I have gone to and seen an innocent looking dog sitting there with their owner standing next to them. This dog's owner has a look of total dismay on their face. They have tried everything they could think of to correct the problem they're having with their dog to no avail. All of their efforts have been thwarted. They love their dog like a family member, yet it's hard to come home day after day to find their home and/or their belongings destroyed.

Oftentimes these owners are at a breaking point. The relationship with their dog is fractured. And the dog that is both guilty as charged yet innocent of being able to grasp the full scope of the situation somehow knows that I am there to help. And help them I will.

I am grateful to share my extensive experience as a dog trainer and behavior management specialist with you. What I need you to do is to listen to your heart as you read my words. In this book I will explore the possible causes of your dog's destructive behavior and give you tangible solutions that you can implement right away.

Some of the information and stories will be interesting, but may not apply to your dog's situation. But then you will read something that strikes a chord and you will know: "That's it, that's us, that's my dog!"

Likewise, certain management solutions and tools may feel right for your situation while others just won't. You get to choose.

THE INTEGRATED APPROACH

All teachers teach through stories. As you read on you will be introduced to a new way of thinking and training, The Integrated Approach. The Integrated Approach to dog training is unique because it combines spirituality and the sciences of psychology and etiology. Just as Integrative Medicine takes into account the whole person, so does The Integrated Approach to dog training take into account the whole dog: mind, body and spirit. The Integrated Approach to dog training views the dog first and foremost as a kindred spirit.

The principals of behavior modification that govern human behavior are equally applicable to dog behavior. The Integrated Approach to dog training reminds dog owners that innate behaviors are a part of a dog's Divine nature. Instinctive behaviors in dogs, such as jumping for joy, barking or chewing, should never be thought of as being bad in and of themselves. Rather these are inherent behaviors that oftentimes require management strategies.

The definition of the word integrated is: to combine diverse elements into a harmonious whole. Whether one is discussing dog training equipment, methods of training, or the use of positive and negative reinforcement, The Integrated Approach to dog training is designed to be open and inclusive rather than exclusive.

Both people and dogs are unique regardless of race or breed. There is no one-size-fits-all. The Integrated Approach to dog training is always flexible, seeking effective solutions that are for the greatest good in each unique situation. Once again, this book will offer you an excellent example of diverse solutions for various situations.

My greatest challenges in this lifetime have also provided me with my greatest gifts. I have learned to believe in and rely on God, the Divine, with everything

I do. It is only fitting then that I incorporate the concept of The Integrated Approach to dog training into the upcoming sections of this book.

A brief overview of the three sections:

Section One: Separation Anxiety vs. Containment Phobia

As the title suggests, in "Separation Anxiety Versus Containment Phobia" the specific traits of these two conditions will be discussed. I will clearly compare how these two conditions are similar and how they are different.

> Containment Phobia Is Almost Always
> Misdiagnosed as Separation Anxiety

These two conditions have many similarities that have clouded their very distinct differences. The problem with this is that *when a condition is misdiagnosed, there is no cure!*

I will also offer suggestions on how to manage Separation Anxiety and Containment Phobia. Each of these management solutions is as different as are the conditions themselves.

Section Two: Why Is Your Dog Destructive When You're Gone?

In this section I will tear down the myth that **all** destructive behavior that occurs during an owner's absence is due to Separation Anxiety. People are being led to believe that the reason their dog is destructive during their absence is solely because their dog misses them.

Aren't our egos something?
Since it occurs when I'm gone it must be about me!
This Is Not Always the Case!!!

In Section Two I will explore:

1. **Frustrating Factors for Dogs:**
   Using the psychological approach I will examine additional reasons why dogs might find their own life circumstances frustrating. Dogs that are frustrated oftentimes destroy their owner's property during the course of venting their frustrations.

2. **Mismanagement:**
   The dog finds the behavior (the act of destroying whatever it is destroying) fun and rewarding. Some possible reasons for this could be the dog was mismanaged growing up and learned to enjoy doing these things, or it is being mismanaged now.

3. **Thunderstorm Phobia:**
   The dog experiences the sound of thunder as dangerous. The owner's property is destroyed during the dog's attempts to escape the sound.

Section Three: Medicating Our Dogs: Is Taking a Pill the Answer?

Could the solution be that simple? Wouldn't it be lovely if it were!

There are indeed times when medication plays a vital part in managing a dog's behavior and restoring quality of life. Then again, when it is not the solution, that little pill may put false hope in the dog owner's heart and thwart efforts to improve the situation once again.

This section will explore the pros and cons of medicating dogs. I will also share when, *in my opinion*, medicating your dog is the solution.

Finally, I want to promise you that you are about to read new information and gain new insights that you have not read or heard anywhere else. I am a natural when it comes to dog training, but I cannot say the same for myself when it comes to writing books. I need a burning desire to find the discipline to do what it takes to actually write a book. This book is being written with the intention of making a difference in your life as well as in the world.

I pray that with your help, the new insights you gain from reading my words will have an international outreach. With your help we can save dogs' lives, as well as the hearts of the people who love them. Thank you!

Part I
Separation Anxiety Versus Containment Phobia

When I think of a dog experiencing Separation Anxiety, I think of Maria and her little Dapple Dachshund named Duke. The two of them live in a townhouse and have a very strong bond. Maria goes to work each day, leaving Duke with run of the house. Duke is well behaved when she's gone; he doesn't bark or do anything naughty. He's used to this routine, as it's been this way his entire life. But once Maria arrives home in the evening and during the weekends they are inseparable. Actually Maria would like more space from Duke, but he will let out a horrible screeching cry when she goes out of sight for even a minute. Recently Maria and a friend were riding in her car with Duke. Maria stopped at a convenience market to get something. Her passenger, who remained in the car, was horrified, startled and nearly deafened by Duke's screaming which continued until Maria got back. Maria was so embarrassed she'd had enough. They are now coming to see me.

By contrast, there's another dog, Lace, whose behavior and history are also very good examples of a dog experiencing Separation Anxiety (She's actually pictured on page 26). When Lace was a puppy, she was **almost never left alone**. Her owners both worked very long days so they thought it best to hire their daughter to puppy sit while they were gone. This continued until Lace was at least 8 or 9 months of age. When their daughter quit coming, because they thought Lace was now old enough to be left alone, Lace was frustrated … big time! That's when her destructive behavior began.

Separation Anxiety: The Cause

Both the dog owner and the dog experience Separation Anxiety when the bond between them is strong. The stronger the bond, the stronger the experience of Separation Anxiety will be.

The term "Separation Anxiety" was first used to describe the feelings of loss and anxiety that occurred when human beings were separated from each other. We can thank John Bowlby for his work in this area. He was referred to as a psychological evolutionary and is best known for his studies in what he introduced as Attachment Theory. The full theory is published in a trilogy on *Attachment and Loss* (Basic Books, 1969- 1982).

Here's the takeaway: John Bowlby established an ethological theory that our DNA dictates our human need for each other. Not only do humans need and depend on each other, but they may also suffer

Separation Anxiety when binding relationships become unavailable or no longer exist.

The ethological studies regarding canines also prove that dogs are social animals, more commonly referred to as "pack animals." They need each other for their own survival, and this is in their DNA as well.

The Integrated Approach to dog training would sum these studies up by saying they also prove that attachment is a part of the Divine nature of both people and dogs. This is scientific proof that we do need each other!

When does Separation Anxiety in dogs first begin?

Unless you have had a pregnant female dog give birth to a litter of puppies, you may not realize that the first sign of Separation Anxiety in dogs occurs during the puppies' first weeks of life, before the puppies' eyes are even open. When a litter is first born, the mother dog has a natural tendency to stay with the litter constantly. If she's a naturally good mother dog, she won't leave the puppies other than to go relieve herself or to feed herself. There is a magnetic energy of needing to be together every minute, which is really a beautiful sight to see.

Even during these first few weeks, when the mother dog leaves the whelping box, the puppies oftentimes join in a song of crying out, calling for her to return. Even though the song did not begin the instant she left, once the litter realizes they are getting hungry without her, the chorus will begin and continue until she comes back to feed them. So crying out for their mother's return begins at a very young age. A puppy's first experience of Separation Anxiety occurs early and at its root is an innate need for self-preservation.

Then somewhere between 4 and 5 weeks of age those puppies begin getting their first set of needle sharp puppy teeth. The value of these sharp baby teeth is that it encourages mother dog to wean them and the puppies begin learning to rely on another food source. It's at this point that the mother dog's owner and the mother dog begin to share responsibility for the litter. This is also the point when the puppy learns to imprint upon and depend more upon their relationship with people.

Both human beings and dogs experience love and Separation Anxiety because both are a part of our Divine natures. The closer the relationship between human and dog, the more likely the diagnosis of Separation Anxiety is correct. **To have an accurate diagnosis that a dog's destructive behavior is as a result of Separation Anxiety one must also have the insight that there is a very close relationship between the owner and dog and that the dog's destructive behavior is solely an expression of frustration as a result of being separated or left alone.**

"Anything Nice Has a Price"

Robert Schuller, Crystal Cathedral Ministries

Recently I met a new client, a senior woman who was probably in her late 70's or early 80's. She had just gotten a new puppy after not being a dog owner for over 30 years. She had always liked dogs, but her last husband of some 30 years did not, so she chose to live without. Prior to that, both while growing up and when she was living with her first husband, she did have dogs. She referred to her dogs as "ranch dogs" and the ranches she was referring to consisted of 10,000 acres.

I assisted her with housebreaking her new puppy, which was something she had never done before. I remember her looking me straight in the eye and saying, "You know, ranch dogs don't want to come inside!" This was such an unusual statement to hear that I asked her to repeat it one more time. She said, "Yeah, you can't get a ranch dog to come inside. And when you do they just want to go back out again."

I was delighted to be reminded of this perspective. I knew what she was talking about. As a child growing up in Iowa, my grandparents had "farm dogs" and the same would have been true for most of them. Farmers didn't bring the dogs inside. They would create a nice warm bed for their dogs in the barn with the other animals. Similarly, these farms were hundreds if not thousands of acres in size, and the dogs could run free. Plus, at that time, there were no leash laws.

Based on these experiences, ranch dogs and farm dogs would not likely experience Separation Anxiety from people. They would, however, experience Separation Anxiety from their free-range outdoor environment because it was what they knew and loved and where they felt most at home.

Separation Anxiety: The Effect

Your dog has a reason for doing what it is doing!

Dogs experience frustration when life presents them with circumstances they find unpleasant. Being left home alone suddenly may be very upsetting to a dog **that is not accustomed to it**.

When a dog is frustrated because of Separation Anxiety, it will most likely vent its frustrations through one or more of the following innate behaviors while the owner is away:

1. Excessive or destructive chewing.
2. Vocalizing by howling or excessive barking.
3. Excessive digging.
4. Soiling in the house. Defecating is symptomatic of frustration.
5. Self-Mutilation / Self Harm

Are dogs spiteful?
To answer this question accurately, I believe one only has to look into the heart and soul of the dog. For many of us, the dog has been our greatest example of unconditional love here on earth. It's also safe to say that ...

Unconditional Love and Spitefulness Cannot Occupy the Same Space

It's understandable that people might jump to the conclusion that the dog is behaving out of spite. After all, this is a human trait. The distinction I am making here is that yes, a dog can be frustrated about something and, yes, a dog can vent its frustrations, but when it does, it is not thinking, *Darn them, I'll get even.* Instead the dog would more likely be thinking, *I'm upset and I need to vent.* Venting is also a means of coping for dogs.

It is important for you to understand the difference here so that you can deal with the situation at hand in a more objective manner. It's only human to dislike the destructive behavior your dog exhibits, but it's vital that you find forgiveness in your heart for your dog. There is undisciplined discipline that is governed by anger. Love and respect is the foundation of any healthy relationship. Disciplined discipline is based on love.

Behavior Never Lies!

Here are some examples of the type of destruction to home and property that is the effect of Separation Anxiety. This is what can happen when a dog rummages through household items, venting frustration as a means of coping. When you compare this sampling to the photos of the effect of Containment Phobia, the photos will demonstrate the distinct difference. In this case, a picture is worth a thousand words.

Destruction to home and property

Self-Mutilation / Self-Harm

This section is without photos though I have no doubt that you can visualize a sore on a dog's foot, hip, or tail as a result of chewing on itself out of frustration from being left alone. Usually this behavior would be diagnosed as allergy related, but it could also be an effect of Separation Anxiety.

Containment Phobia: The Cause

Containment Phobia is defined as an extreme fear of being trapped. The ethological study of wolf behavior will confirm that the wolf will go to great extremes to escape any environment in which it feels trapped. This self-preservation response or Containment Phobic response is imbedded in the wolf's DNA and Divine nature.

With this book I will establish a formal theory that dogs, which are descendants of the wolf, are prone to experience the same level of Containment Phobia as their ancestors. Certain dogs have inherited this condition in their DNA and it is a part of their Divine nature as well.

Containment Phobia can show up in any breed and the behavior speaks for itself. Because of this distinct inherent difference from Separation Anxiety, the solutions for managing Containment Phobia are different as well.

Author's Experience

I've been a professional dog trainer since 1977. Since that time I have encountered numerous incidents of Containment Phobia in both wolves and dogs. My extensive experience has allowed me to become an expert in this area.

One of my earliest influences was author and professional dog trainer, William Koehler. He was the author of the bestselling book, <u>The Koehler Method of Guard Dog Training</u>. He was also a very influential industry professional from the 1960's through the mid 1980's.

William Koehler played a significant role in the history of dog training, though many present day trainers now criticize his methods.

His career began in the military, where he worked with military protection dogs and was instrumental in the development of their protection training programs. His book, <u>The Koehler Method of Guard Dog Training</u>, was a byproduct of his military dog training experience. But this bestselling book influenced not only how dog owners thought, but also how dog trainers taught and how breeders bred. There was a balance between supply and demand.

In the mid 70's many Americans were transitioning from rural to urban living, crime was still relatively new in the news, and as a result many were appalled at the idea that they now needed to lock their doors when they left their homes. Dog owners wanted their own personal protection dogs to protect their homes and property.

Breeders of German Shepherds and Dobermans were at their peak during this time. Also, the Rottweiler and Shar Pei were just starting to be imported into the United States.

I know that as a dog trainer, I was training more Dobermans and German Shepherds than any other breeds. Most of the phone calls to the dog training business where I was first employed were from people wanting obedience training first and then protection training. In the 1970's and on into the1980's, protection training was as popular and as commonplace as agility training is today.

Now that you have a historic context for this period in dog training history, there is one other fad / phase that you should know about that was also occurring. For a relatively short period in time, the wolf (*canis lupus*) also became one of the most popular sought after pets. The fact that today we still have more wolf hybrids in the United States than any other country is reminiscent of this period.

What fueled the intrigue? In part, many thought that this exotic animal, the wolf, with its size and stature, would certainly be a deterrent to crime and a great personal protection dog; this turned out not to be the case.

Another very unique characteristic of the wolf that some breeders found attractive was the fact that a pure wolf is free from any hip dysplasia. Hip dysplasia was, and still is, a huge concern in the breeding of German Shepherds. So it wasn't long before *some* German Shepherd dog breeders who were looking for a more massive and healthy protection dog started using wolves in their breeding programs.

Then in 1983 Walt Disney released the movie "Never Cry Wolf." In this movie a biologist documents wolf behavior as he develops a strong bond to the *canis lupus*. I believe that this movie also fueled the interest and idealistic view of owning a pure wolf.

By the mid 1980's, I had a substantial number of clients with either pure wolves or a very high percentage of wolf hybrids in their breeding. These clients were all dealing with the same problems inherent with raising and living with the *canis lupus*. The challenges were extreme and required a huge commitment from the owner. The behaviors they needed to manage were rooted in the very DNA of the wolf. This was my first "real life" introduction to the fact that while innate behaviors are manageable, it is foolish to think we can extinguish, eliminate, or cure them. I had to learn how to work with Mother Nature.

The most difficult behavior to manage, which threatened this animal's health and safety, and contributed to the destruction of the owners' home and property, centered on the fact that a true wolf demonstrates a phobic reaction to being contained.

A wolf has an extreme innate fear of being trapped.
Being trapped is experienced as life threatening!!!

Unlike today, during this time period *most* people would leave a puppy outdoors in a natural environment as a means of managing puppy behavior when they were gone. In Tucson, Arizona, most of my client's homes had a fenced yard and the leash law was being enforced in the city limits.

Rather than coming home to a happy puppy that had been allowed its freedom all day, owners of wolf hybrid pups were coming home to find incidents of destructive behavior. It would usually begin with scratch marks on the backdoor that led into the house. Upon closer inspection, they would also find holes along their fence where their pup was attempting to dig out. Similarly, the back gate was also scratched up. In fact, the back gate was usually the first place their pup would successfully dig under and escape.

This happened consistently AND it didn't matter how "big" the backyard was. As the pup grew, so did the damage to the backdoor, the fence, and the back gate.

To make things even worse, these wolf/wolf hybrid pups were injuring themselves in the process. When the gates and fence were strong enough to keep the pup contained, the pup would then, out of necessity, discover its ability to climb and/or jump over the fence.

Necessity Gives Birth to Creativity in Dogs!

Another peculiar attribute of these behaviors, which spoke volumes, was the fact that many of these animals did not run away once they had escaped the backyard. It was commonplace for the owner to come home and find their wolf/wolf hybrid pup sitting on the front porch awaiting their return. This animal didn't want to leave, it just couldn't stand the idea of being trapped or contained.

After all attempts to keep the pup safely in their backyard proved futile, the owner's next logical step was to keep this same animal in the house when they were gone. Matters only grew worse!

Most people would begin by leaving their wolf/wolf hybrid pup in the laundry room with the door shut. The door had to be shut because they already knew that a doggy gate would only be a temporary stumbling block. Unfortunately, those who tried this method of containment ended up with the same results. The doors would be scratched and chewed, the doorframes would be destroyed, and oftentimes the wall next to the door would have gaping holes. It was also quite common that the pup would defecate in the area, and then spread it throughout the room. And it was not uncommon to find blood on the floor and walls, as injury was often a result of this behavior.

Shutting the wolf/wolf hybrid pup in a bedroom resulted in the same type of destruction mentioned above, but with the addition of destroyed window coverings. Sometimes the carpet was "dug up" next to the door where the pup tried to get out.

When given freedom of the entire house, destruction still occurred in association with attempts to escape the house. And it didn't matter how "big" the house was either. The behavior was specific and direct. The wolf/wolf hybrid pup has an innate fear of being trapped. All of its destructive behavior occurred as a result of trying to escape.

All Dogs Are Descendants of the Wolf

In today's world, I believe that the condition of Containment Phobia surfaces in approximately 10 to 15 percent of our dog population. That may not sound like a huge percentage, but when you think of the number of dogs that are on the planet, it's a large number of dogs.

The Profile of the Containment Phobic Dog

Breeds
It is neither breed nor gender specific.

Size of dog
It is present in all sizes of dogs from toy to giant. The smaller dog may not choose fence jumping or attacking windows as an escape route for obvious reasons.

Age of dog
Phobias tend to show up with age. Containment Phobia in dogs may show up early in the puppy's development, or the onset of the condition may be postponed until approximately six months of age.

Temperament of dog
Some of the calmest and best-behaved dogs suffer from Containment Phobia. Often this is the only behavior problem the owner has with this dog.

Shelters
Dogs that have Containment Phobia are very likely to end up at shelters. Whether the previous owner finally gives up in despair and relinquishes the dog because they cannot keep them contained or the dog escapes and gets lost then found, these dogs are more likely to end up at shelters.

The Client Interview

The following is a sample script of a conversation between a dog training behaviorist and a dog owner. The dog owner has called for help, as she has a dog that is destructive when she's gone. This Client Interview illustrates a typical scenario of questions and answers that lead the behaviorist to conclude that this dog suffers from Containment Phobia.

The initial phone call:
Dog Owner: My dog is destructive in the house when I am gone. If I can't fix this problem fast, I may have to get rid of him because he is destroying my home.

Dog Trainer: I would like to schedule a private lesson with you at your home so that I can see firsthand what's going on, and we can design a training program to provide you with solutions.

An appointment is scheduled, and the dog trainer goes to the home for a lesson, not knowing what kind of destruction is taking place.

Dog Owner: I'm so glad you could come out right away. I have to go to work on Monday and I can't continue leaving this dog at home. He's destroying my house.

Dog Trainer: Let's begin by having you show me what the dog is destroying.

Dog Owner: I'll start with the laundry room. We have been putting him in here with the door shut. Look at what he does! The molding next to the door is destroyed, the door is destroyed, and he has even dug up the flooring in front of the door.

Dog Trainer: Did you ever try leaving him in this area with a dog gate instead of closing the door?

Dog Owner: Oh, he has been jumping over dog gates since he was a puppy. When he was a puppy we limited him to the kitchen area instead of giving him the run of the house and he would jump right over the gate.

Dog Trainer: Did you ever try using a crate?

Dog Owner: Sure, the breeder told us to use a crate, so we got one right away. He hated it!

Dog Trainer: How do you know he hated it? What did he do?

Dog Owner: Well, at first we had him take naps in it if we were home. That went fine. The breeder also suggested that we feed him in the crate so he would have an additional reason to like it. We did that, too! Since he would jump dog gates, I tried leaving him in the crate for short periods when I went to work. I would come home at lunch to let him out, but he would still have no part of it. He chewed through the first plastic crate in two days. Then we bought a metal crate. Do you want to see what he did to that?

Dog Trainer: Sure.

Dog Owner: Look at this! He literally bent the bars. That, of course, took him a few days. The first day I came home for lunch he had defecated in the crate, which is something I was told dogs never do. The next day, I thought he had urinated in the crate, but it was drool. Then he started tearing at the metal bars, and I was afraid he was going to hurt himself so we just started leaving him outside. We have a nice big fenced backyard.

Dog Trainer: Good! Why don't you show me the backyard?

Dog Owner: Look, it's almost half an acre! You'd think he would be happy. Actually he was fine for a while. Then he started trying to dig out under the gate. You can see where he has scratched it, so my husband poured cement under it. The next thing we knew he started jumping the 6-foot wall, so we can't leave him outside anymore. **He doesn't go anywhere; he just jumps the fence and waits by the front door.** However, animal control came by and gave us a citation.

Dog Trainer: Let's go back inside and you can show me what else he has destroyed.

Dog Owner: We have been leaving him in the laundry room when we are gone, but last week he somehow managed to open the door and get out. He attacked the blinds at the front window, attacked the curtains by the kitchen window, and scratched up the front door. That is when I called you. We just can't go on living like this.

Dog Trainer: How old is he?

Dog Owner: He is going to be a year-and-a-half this month. It just doesn't make sense to me. What is the matter with this dog? Dogs are supposed to love their crate and he hates it. Dogs are never supposed to soil in their crate and he did. We have never scolded him in the aftermath; we know better than that. We exercise and walk him every day. He has everything a dog could want.

Dog Trainer: How is he when you are at home?

Dog Owner: He's the perfect dog. My husband and I both just love him or we would never have put up with all of this. He is as calm as can be. He is good with people and great with our grandchildren.

Crate Training

It seems fitting to discuss crate training at this point. The concept of crate training was also a new trend in the 1970's. It was not an easy sell for dog owners. Why cage when you could let a dog live in a natural environment like the outdoors?

So the analogy was created that it would be the dog's own personal space and that they would love it just like a wolf loves its den. We can all comprehend this comparison, but in reality it's like comparing apples to oranges. **A wolf's den has an open door policy.** A wolf chooses this residence to shelter it from unpleasant weather conditions and to find safety from predators.

For the wolf/wolf hybrid owners who tried using a crate, they came home to either:

a. So much drool it was hard to tell if it was drool or urine.
b. A destroyed crate.
c. A pup that had escaped the crate and was free in the house.
d. A pup that may have injured itself in the process of trying to escape.
e. Neighbors complaining about the howling.

The Crate Was <u>Never</u> an Option - A wolf has an extreme innate fear of being trapped.

Being trapped is experienced as life threatening!!!

Behavior Modification Techniques
Cannot Alter What Nature Has Created.
Regression Is Always Predictable!

The Sisters: Claustrophobia and Containment Phobia

Claustrophobia is defined as a fear of confined spaces. Dogs, like people who suffer from Claustrophobia, experience panic and an accelerated heart rate. People sweat while dogs pant and drool.

An example of this would be a Claustrophobic dog left in a crate.

At first its owner might think it had urinated in the crate when in fact it hadn't; there was just that much drool.

Containment Phobia is defined as a fear of being trapped. When dogs are unable to move freely from one residential environment to another, **regardless of the size of the space,** they panic.

An example of this would be a Containment Phobic dog left at a typical residential property. A dog with Containment Phobia that is locked outside in the backyard with no one home may destroy the house trying to get in or jump the wall or destroy the fence and/or gate trying to get out. This same dog is capable of equivalent damage when locked inside a house and attempting to escape to the outside. It is not the size of the space that frightens them; it is being trapped or contained in an area.

Mild to Extreme

The truth is, God created each person and each dog as an individual, regardless of the person's race or the dog's breed. The dog is powerless when experiencing the condition of Claustrophobia or Containment Phobia. **The level of frustration a dog experiences is very individual.** I think of it in terms of drawing a line representing a continuum that goes from mild to extreme. The root of the fear once again is a fear of being trapped.

Claustrophobia Mild	Containment Phobia More Extreme
An innate need for an expansive area.	An innate need for freedom of movement from inside to outside.

Mild to Severe Cases

A dog's response to Containment Phobia may seem mild at first, but just like Thunderstorm Phobia, Containment Phobia will become more severe with repetition and age. **It is not the age of the dog that makes the experience and the dog's response more violent, but rather conditioning elevated by the repetition that comes with age.**

A Claustrophobic dog may not have Containment Phobia. However, a Containment Phobic dog is almost always Claustrophobic as well.

It should also be noted that a dog is also capable of experiencing all three conditions: Claustrophobia, Containment Phobia and Separation Anxiety. **The diagnosis is determined according to behavior.**

Case Study of Claustrophobia

Background Information: The following is a summary of key points that allowed me to draw the conclusion of Claustrophobia. If you are a dog training behaviorist you may be thinking of additional detailed questions that one would ask before drawing conclusions. I did not include the entire interview of everything I asked over an hour-and-a-half lesson here, but trust me, I asked.

Client: Female senior citizen who lives alone. **Dog:** Recently adopted 2-year-old male Great Dane.

Concern: My client moved to a new house and adopted a dog at the same time. When I arrived she was still unpacking and had only had the dog for a short time. My first impression of the dog was that it was a fabulous dog with a great disposition. It seemed to be the perfect companion for her, except for the fact that she couldn't leave him alone. He broke out of confined areas and defecated in the house. Once again, this dog never urinated in the house. He only had a bowel movement when he was left home alone. *She had described her situation to her veterinarian over the phone and he concluded that her dog suffered from Separation Anxiety and was not housebroken.* Fortunately he also recommended that she talk to a dog training behaviorist, me.

Housebreaking Behavior

What I learned at the first appointment was that the client walks the dog twice a day. And the dog never soiled in the house when she was home. The dog wouldn't defecate in her small back yard at her house. It wouldn't defecate when he was on leash either. He waited until she walked him to a large fenced-in area available to residents and let him off leash. Then, like clockwork, he had a bowel movement twice a day.

Conclusion: This dog WAS housebroken. This was a clean dog! In general, dogs consider their bowel movement to be foul, especially compared to urine. (Once again, I'm speaking in general terms for the purposes of this case study.) He didn't want to have a bowel movement in a small back yard or on leash because he had a need to be able to defecate and then get far away from it. When he was on leash he felt too close to the owner and he needed more space to be comfortable. *Therefore, when this same dog defecated in the house in the owner's absence, it was purely an expression of being upset*. It was a means for him to vent.

Story Continues: Of course the owner was upset and wondered if she should return this dog to the rescue group. She needed to go places and *she believed that the dog was upset because she was leaving*. **Wrong!** I had to burst that bubble and explain that, first of all, it was not Separation Anxiety and it was not about missing her. The dog demonstrated this behavior immediately upon adoption and prior to having any kind of time to develop an attachment to her. This was already an established behavior or habit that he brought with him.

First Clue: The first confined space she tried to leave him in was a large wire crate. *He consistently broke out of the crate!* After he broke out, he found himself with access to only a small portion of the house and **yet** *he did not expand his escape attempts by attacking the exits such as doors and windows*. No, he just needed to escape the small space and then he defecated. Defecating under these circumstances could be compared to a human being having a good cry after a trauma. *Naturally, the client was confused because everyone knows that if a dog soils in the house you need to minimize their space to control it, right? WRONG! Not always!*

Next, she decided to confine him to her relatively small kitchen. The same thing happened. He escaped the kitchen. *In this case I noticed she had windows in the kitchen and once again he didn't target the windows*. He was motivated to escape the small kitchen and get into the rest of the house. Again he defecated, but it was in her living room. There was never any destruction other than the destruction that occurred in the process of trying to escape.

The Cure Was Two-Fold
First: We gave him the entire house in the client's absence and did not close off any doors. She never

crated him again. Since this dog was Claustrophobic, which is an innate behavior, we knew the behavior was never going away. I did not suggest desensitization techniques to help this dog adjust to the crate because they are misleading to the client and they give false hope. There is no sense arguing with Mother Nature: You will lose!

Second: I taught this client a healing exercise for her dog: **Leaving and Returning**. A human being, a mother for example, can tell her child that she will be back soon. A dog, on the other hand, learns from experience and they need to experience Leaving and Returning. This healing exercise is good for all of the conditions being discussed in this book: Separation Anxiety, Claustrophobia, and Containment Phobia.

Most dogs begin venting their frustration about being left alone within the first 30 minutes after the owner walks out the door. The goal of this healing exercise is to leave and return enough times, over short periods of random times (5mins, 10mins, 5mins, 10mins, 5mins, 15mins, 7mins, 15mins, 5mins, 20mins - working your way up to 40mins), so at the end of the day, the dog thinks, *"Alright already, I got it. You leave and you come back. It's no big deal and nothing bad happens to me. Stay gone already, I'm tired of getting up."* This technique is also known as "flooding" in behavioral terms.

Result: The client called me on several occasions saying she still couldn't believe it! Not one single accident since our lesson and no destruction. Life is grand. Lesson learned is that we get our needs fulfilled when we fulfill the needs of another. THIS WAS NOT SEPARATION ANXIETY.

This Was a Case of a Wonderful Dog with a Mild Case of Claustrophobia
Behavior Never Lies!

Early Signs of Containment Phobia
Early signs of Containment Phobia are claustrophobic reactions when left in a crate. This same puppy is also more likely to scramble to jump over a gate when contained in a room.

Escape behaviors include:

- Ongoing attempts to break out of a dog crate.
- Jumping over or going through dog gates.
- Climbing out of exercise pens.
- An ability to open doors with lever door handles.
- Destroying exits when contained in a room. This could include: doors, windows, window coverings (such as curtains and/or blinds), etc.
- Chewing through leashes when used as a means of containment.
- When sufficiently contained in the back yard, destroying the entryways into the house trying to get back in.
- Ongoing attempts to escape kennel runs.
- Jumping a fence.
- Digging underneath a fence.

- Chewing through a fence or wall.
- Chipping teeth on a chain link fence trying to escape.
- Breaking through glass windows.

It should also be noted that once the Containment Phobic dog does manage to escape, it is also less likely to run away. Commonly the owner will come home to find the dog sitting on the front porch.

Expert Experience – John C. Fentress, PhD.

John C. Fentress, PhD. author, lecturer, and scientist

Next I would like to introduce you to John C. Fentress, PhD. John was the founding member of Wild Canid Survival and Research Center in St. Louis Missouri in 1972. The purpose of this Research Center was to give wolves a habitat. His experience also included working at the animal behavior lab at the Cambridge University of England as well as working with over 50 wolves at the Canadian Center for Wolf Research in Nova Scotia.

In essence John dedicated much of his life's work, over 30 years, to studying the behavioral development, communication and personality traits of wolves. In his most recent book, to be released in 2015, John shares numerous stories of lessons he learned from Lupey, a wolf he raised from the time it was a young pup. John was only 24 years old when he first got Lupey at the age of 4 ½ weeks - he even had to bottle-feed him.

John's firsthand experience with Containment Phobia confirms that pure wolves have an innate phobic reaction to being trapped, or what they consider to be trapped. His own wolf Lupey once dug through the plaster of a bedroom wall to get out of the bedroom. John's memoir of Lupey includes these stories of Lupey's need to escape confinement.

You may visit his website at **www.LupeyWolf.com**.

Enjoy my interview with John Fentress by going to **www.DestructiveDogs.com/JohnFentress**

Containment Phobia: The Effect

Behavior Never Lies!

The following pictures demonstrate clearly the type of destructive behavior that should be recognized and categorized as Containment Phobia.

Destruction to Home & Property

Self-Mutilation / Self-Harm

It is not uncommon for Containment Phobic dogs to bloody their paws in the process of trying to escape confinement. However, the most common and permanent damage is usually done to their canine teeth.

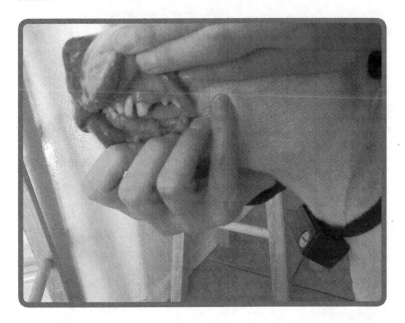

Broken canine teeth (as seen in the picture above) are most often the result of either:

a. Chewing on chain link fence to escape.
b. Playing with rocks (which would be totally unrelated).

The Comparison Conclusion: Separation Anxiety Versus Containment Phobia

1. The conclusion is that these two conditions are both inherent. The Integrated Approach to Dog Training would suggest that this serves the dog's Divine need for self-preservation. The scientific approach prefers words such as the ethological need for self-preservation.

2. As innate conditions, both are permanent.

3. Both conditions have varying levels of intensity ranging from mild to extreme.

4. Both conditions are manageable.

5. The effects of both conditions will be acted out during the owner's absence.

6. The destructive behavior associated with Separation Anxiety will be found either within the home or outside in the yard.

7. The destructive behavior associated with Containment Phobia will be directed towards home furnishings that either prevent the dog from entering or exiting the home environment.

8. **The behavior modification approach to managing Separation Anxiety is entirely different from the behavior modification strategies for managing Containment Phobia.**

9. The only solution that would work for both conditions is to never leave the dog home alone.

10. **Separation Anxiety and Containment Phobia are two distinctly different conditions and must be treated as such.**

Managing Separation Anxiety

This segment is about sharing new insights and management strategies that will encourage a healthy relationship between dog owners and their dogs.

We understand that Separation Anxiety is an innate quality and that it may actually ensure a dog's survival in this world. The experience can have a positive outcome. For example, when a mother dog hears her litter crying out and she returns to feed them. On the other hand, when a dog's experience borders on being traumatic, that information is embedded in its subconscious in the form of a traumatic memory that can influence its reaction in a more negative way the next time. **What is learned can always be relearned, but if we can avoid unnecessary trauma and/or prevent it in the first place then it makes sense to do so.**

BEFORE Your Puppy First Arrives Home

There are many occasions when a dog owner is in contact with either the breeder or the foster parents that are raising the litter of puppies from where your puppy will come. How a puppy is raised and managed during those initial weeks prior to you receiving the puppy could make a huge difference in the ease of the transition from its first home to yours. Whenever possible, it's ideal to soften a separation transition and reduce the likelihood of Separation Anxiety.

Things the breeder or foster parent could do to reduce the likelihood of the puppies having a traumatic experience as they are separated from their littermates and are taken away to their new home:

- Remove the puppy from its mother and littermates often to have one-on-one time learning to socialize with a human being. The fact that it will be returned to its littermates helps ease the adjustment.

- Crate training is a very practical and necessary tool for many dog owners. When the breeder or foster parents can begin crate training prior to the puppy arriving at its new home it eases the transition. They could begin crate training by feeding the puppies in individual crates as well as letting them nap in crates by themselves. They could also put the puppies in crates with something very rewarding to chew on. It's ideal if the puppies are facing each other and see that their littermates are close by. If one puppy is particularly stressed, two puppies can be put in the crate together. This should be a gentle transition training.

- **Take the puppies for car rides.** Most carsickness is actually caused by stress and trauma rather than motion sickness. Being removed from their first home and their littermates could be a traumatic experience for a puppy. If and when a puppy associates this traumatic event with the car ride it, it can leave deep-seeded anxiety that may also contribute to carsickness.

- Keep the puppies until they are between 7 to 8 weeks of age.

NOTE: The ideal time for a puppy to be removed from its littermates and go to its new forever home is between 7 and 8 weeks of age. No sooner and no later. A common misconception from backyard breeders who don't know any better is that the puppies can be released as early as 5 to 6 weeks of age. They will tell the new owners that since the puppy is eating on its own, it can go home now. They are WRONG! Even though the puppies don't require their mother to feed them, they still need to remain with their littermates to learn normal social behavior as they grow accustomed to being without their mother dog.

If you did end up with a puppy that didn't have the perfect puppy beginnings, it just means that you may need to step up your efforts to socialize them with other puppies once you get them.

You Have a New Puppy, Now What?

What can you, the new dog owner, do to transition the puppy into its new home environment? You can make the difference in whether the transition is smooth or traumatic. It's not uncommon to hear that people begin crate training right away. This may be ideal if the breeder had already introduced crate training. **It's also not uncommon to hear that the puppy cried all through the night its first night of being isolated in a crate. Not a great way to begin crate training nor is it a way to avoid what could be experienced as traumatic Separation Anxiety as a result of being isolated.**

Crate training is a great tool *for most puppies*, helping their owners to housebreak them and manage other behaviors like teething when the owner can't be around. The crate may also be a necessary tool for a dog when traveling, going to the groomers and sometimes the veterinarian's office. It's important to introduce it correctly and not abuse it.

Crate Training Begins with You at Home

Overnight

It's best to ease a new puppy into the fact that life has taken a dramatic turn. It's just a puppy after all. I think it's always best to allow the puppy to sleep near you where they can see you and alert you should they need to be let out to go potty. Their crate could either be on a nightstand, next to your bed, or you may want to consider a soft Sherpa Bag, which you could actually put in bed with you. The Sherpa Bag is most ideal for small dogs that will also have a use for it throughout their life.

SHERPA
ORIGINAL DELUXE
www.SherpaPet.com

Learning to sleep in the crate next to you overnight is also a nice way to teach the puppy that when they go in the crate, it's just time to rest.

Additional ways of making the crate a positive experience for your puppy:

a. Feed the puppy its meals in the crate.

b. Keep the crate in areas where the puppy hangs out when you are home. Leave the door open so it can go in and out freely.

c. Let the puppy discover treats and new toys in their crate.

d. Remember that dogs learn by experience. The puppy needs to experience going in and out of the crate as something fun. Many people will use words like "kennel up" as a command for going in, and "ok" for being released to come out. A fun lesson to reinforce this experience might be:

   1. Hold on to your puppy, throw a treat or a very rewarding toy in the crate and then release them with the words "kennel up" and watch the puppy shoot into the crate.

   2. Hold the door closed behind them for a moment and then swing the door open saying "ok" allowing them to come right back out. A lot of verbal praise should be reward enough for coming out. (Save the treat and/or the toy for going in.)

e. When the puppy is ready for a nap, let him nap in the crate with the door closed.

f. Gradually build up the length of time that you leave the puppy in the crate when you are home. Start with very short periods of time (a few minutes) then increase the time. It's really important that you know the puppy has eliminated before you start extending the time. Deliberately leave the room the crate is in and then return, preferably when the puppy is quiet.

g. Refrain from opening the crate door to let the puppy out if it is fussing. **(Unless of course there's a possibility that they do need to potty.)** You want to reward good behavior, which means opening the door to come out either as soon as or once they have been quiet for a little while.

Like any tool, over-using the crate can make it an object to dread. A young puppy should never be left in a crate for more than a few hours. I often meet people who have their more mature puppy with good bladder control in its crate for 8 hours each night plus 8 hours each day. Overusing the crate as a tool will have negative consequences! If this sounds like your situation, then you want to find an alternative form of containment for either overnight, or during the day when you're gone.

Overusing the crate, or any one single confinement tool, can contribute to a dog experiencing Separation Anxiety. The dog learns to associate dreading your departure because they feel punished because they spend **too much** time in a single environment.

When you pair the dread of being shut up with your departure, it may make your departure more traumatic.

Final Note: If it seems that your puppy is not crate trainable, you may have that special puppy which is Containment Phobic, in which case you may want to jump ahead to the section on Managing Containment Phobia (page77).

During the Daytime

During the daytime most puppies are going to need to be left alone in a safe area and they are going to need to cry some. There's a narrow path of "darned if you do and darned if you don't" at this point. One thing is for sure, you don't want to reward crying just because they don't want to be left alone. It's healthy for the puppy to make the adjustment and learn to be more independent.

When You Give Your Puppy Its First Alone Times

Food or something wonderful to chew on is innately rewarding for a dog. Pairing your departures and puppy alone time with food rewards and chew toys is an excellent association. Hopefully the puppy will busy itself to the point of exhaustion and just fall into a nice sleep in your absence.

A tired puppy is more likely to fall asleep. Taking walks **around your property will not only begin boundary training,** but it will tire the puppy and prepare it for some alone time as well.

Reward Puppy's Alone Time With:

a. Kong toys stuffed with a yummy recipe. You can go to **http://www.KongCompany.com** to get some great recipes, which also add variety to your puppy's diet.
b. A great little bone of some sort that they absolutely cannot consume yet will find delightful.
c. Any other safe toy that holds their interest.

Like a baby, you have to be careful about answering their cries for your return even at this age. Did they just wake up and need to go outside? If so, answer the call. Or did you just have them outside? If you know they have been fed and they just don't want to be left alone, then this may be the time to help them learn self-sufficiency and not answer their call for constant companionship. It's vital and healthy for a dog to learn to be self-sufficient.

If you do have a puppy that screams for your constant attention, it does not mean you are supposed to give it to them. You might find a safe daycare situation with other young puppies and let your puppy learn to be comfortable without constant human interaction. Learning to play with other puppies and coexist in a stable pack will help wean it from being too dependent on you right away. **You will also bring home a tired puppy at the end of the day that will be more content when left alone.**

Owners who work all day and need to leave their puppy outside in a safe yard (weather permitting) either by themselves or with other family dogs, actually end up being quite stable and independent dogs. These dogs are also less likely to experience Separation Anxiety from their human parents.

How old was your dog when you first got it? You may have missed these important stages. The person you got your dog from may have done everything wrong. *Shoulda ... Coulda ... Woulda ...* Such is Life. It's time to move on. Remember, what is learned can be relearned.

Developing Healthy Routines

Dogs also benefit from having a routine. A routine is a healthy constant that adds certainty to all of our lives. The opposite of being needy, anxious and uncertain is to be independent, confident and knowing with certainty what to expect.

In order to organize our management strategies into a routine, it may be easiest to think in terms of how we manage our dogs:

A. When we are at home together
B. When we prepare to leave
C. When we are gone
D. When we first return home from being gone
E. Overnight

A. When we are at home together

Encouraging Independence:

It has already been established that dogs that are anxious about being left alone spend a lot of time with their owners when they are home. In fact, the more time a dog spends always with someone, the more difficult it is for it to be left alone.

It's not just about spending time together. The closer the bond between owner and dog, the greater the loss when they are apart. I have always liked the example of how service dogs, which are well obedience-trained dogs and very bonded to their owners, can be some of the worst behaved dogs ever when left alone.

How Is Your Outdoor Area?

It's always interesting to me to hear some people speak about how they believe it's wrong to leave a dog outdoors, even when it's safe and weather permitting. This opinion says more about the feelings of the person than it does about truth or reality.

We are all a reflection of our experiences. If we want a dog to be comfortable being outdoors, then we need to have them spend time outdoors.

Suburban living absolutely requires that dogs be allowed to come inside and spend the majority of their time indoors with the family. But it is still healthy for a dog to be able to spend time outdoors with Mother Nature, whether they are alone or with other family dogs.

So how is your outdoor area? Is it dog friendly? If it's not dog friendly you're more likely to always have your dog inside with you. Could you make some changes to your yard that would make you feel better about encouraging your dog to spend more time outside?

Suggestions / Ideas for Outdoor Independence

If you have a safe yard and the weather is permitting, consider having some fixed outdoor times for your puppy or dog. By fixed I mean there are certain hours where this dog is always outside by itself or with the other family dogs. It could be from 7:00 a.m. to 10:00 a.m. and then again from 2:00 p.m. to 5:00 p.m., just as an example.

The idea here is that your dog will learn there is a routine to when it is outdoors. Having routine times makes being outside more predictable and normal. It will also encourage the dog to accept being alone for periods of time and inevitably the dog will learn to focus on all of the interesting things that go on outside: the noises, the birds, the smells. It's ok to stretch their attention span and to build their independence.

It wasn't all that long ago when it was more the norm for a working family to put the puppy outside at 7:00 a.m. with a bowl of food and water and bring the puppy in when they got home from work at 4:00 or 5:00 p.m. One great thing about dogs raised with this type of routine is that they are more independent and less likely to experience Separation Anxiety. This same dog still has other needs that need to be fulfilled, but there are advantages to such a routine for now.

Some Yards Are Not Dog Friendly and It's Just Not an Option

There are certainly yards that are not safe nor dog friendly. You may find this, for example, in apartment or condo living situations. When the outdoor area is not much larger than a postage stamp and the dog only uses it for a toilet area, it would feel punitive to the dog to be forced to spend any length of time there. So if your yard is not safe or not dog friendly, consider other options.

Client Testimonial

On Their Way to the Dog Park

My Puppy Is So Good!

I can hardly believe how good my German Shepherd puppy is. Currently we live in an apartment with no yard. Since he was 3 months old he has had full run of the house and has yet to ruin anything. We spend an hour at the park in the morning and make a return visit in the evening. In between park times he is at home, alone behaving himself. By filling his needs with both mental and physical exercise, he then allows me to go about my day worry free. We have never used a crate. When it's time to leave him at home alone we'll say "We'll be back buddy" and confidently shut the door without any worries that we will return to a clean home. We expect and trust him to be good!

Suggestions/Ideas for Indoor Independence

When you are at home your dog may be so attached to you that it follows you everywhere. This is a perfect opportunity to encourage your dog to be more independent.

- Having structured crate times would be one way to do this. Structured crate times can encourage independence as well as teach a dog to be at home in the crate. The same could be said about exercise pens or gated off areas in the house.

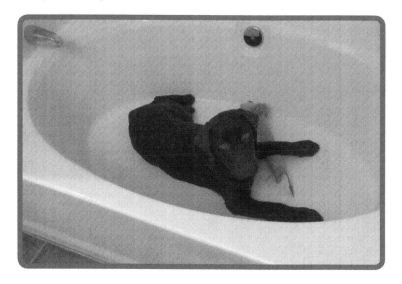

Rocky's mom put him in the tub in her bathroom when she was getting ready for work.

- Having structured times where a dog learns to remain on its dog bed is also beneficial. The best location for the dog's bed should provide it with the ability to see you, but not be underfoot.

In obedience training I have always been a big proponent for tethering a dog on its bed at a distance for four reasons:

1. The dog learns to be independent of you, lying by itself in its own designated area.
2. The dog learns to stay on its bed for a long period of time (1/2 hour to 1 hour), which is useful at other times, such as when company comes or during dinner.
3. The dog learns how to stay on its bed even with a distraction such as you leaving the room. Prior to this it may have only known to follow you everywhere because that was its experience. Now you are providing him with a new experience.
4. Remaining on a dog bed is mental exercise.

Variety is the Spice of Life

We All Need Consistency! We Also Need and Crave Variety!

Your Dog and Exercise

Your dog wants and needs proper exercise either before you go to work and/or after you get home. I have always appreciated how Cesar Milan has been a great proponent for giving a dog exercise.

Remember, a Tired Puppy Is a Happy Puppy

It's not just the exercise that dogs need, but also variety in their routine. **Dogs need to get away from the house and go out in the world.**

The ranch dog and the farm dog that I referred to earlier had hundreds, if not thousands, of acres to wander around on for exercise and mental stimulation. As a result these are also *very stable dogs*. The wolf in the wild has been documented to travel as much as 90 miles a day. I know of no "backyard" that will give a dog that kind of exercise. **And if your dog is getting tons of exercise running up and down the fence barking, stalking people and dogs walking by, then that will become a whole new problem and the topic of my upcoming book, "Dogs That Stalk."**

A trip to the dog park or a day at dog daycare is tremendous for young dogs. *It should also be noted that oftentimes mature, adult dogs might outgrow these forms of recreation.* When your dog accompanies you to run errands or goes for car rides or does anything that gets them out of the house, it will lead to a happier, more stable dog.

A transition we are all witnessing is that as we become more urbanized, the average yard is getting smaller and smaller. Dogs that never go anywhere can be more dangerous. At the same time, we are seeing more dogs out in public than ever before. There is no doubt in my mind that in the next few decades, dogs will become welcome everywhere, much like it is in France and other parts of Europe. The more we, as a society, take our dogs with us wherever we go, the quicker we will become an America where dogs are welcomed everywhere. Many of the dogs that are diagnosed with Separation Anxiety are actually suffering from boredom or cabin fever.

B. When we prepare to leave

Leaving your dog is a fact of life and it's best to treat it is as such.

1. **Even if you are sad about leaving, try your very best not to show it.** Your dog is sensitive to how you feel and if you always feel sad or worried when you leave, then your dog will learn to feel sad and worried about your leaving.

2. When you leave your dog indoors you may want to leave some lights on in addition to the television or radio. The normal sounds your dog always hears when you are home will be comforting when you're gone. For dogs that have great vision and the ability to actually watch TV, I'm a big fan of dog TV. **www.DogTV.com** .

3. A special treat in association with your departure is a great association.

4. A routine of hiding a few treats around the house like an Easter egg hunt can be something your dog will look forward to. They can be hidden indoors or out.

5. Providing your dog with special toys that are not available all of the time can also be a positive association with your departure. The key is to

pick them back up when you come home so that you keep them novel.

6. Dog proof the house before you go – there is no sense in tempting fate. I would consider closing bedroom doors and picking up anything that your dog may be interested in chewing on. Food on the counters should be put away. We don't want to encourage scavenging as a result of boredom. Of course if you feel uncomfortable with giving your dog this much freedom, minimizing the opportunity for destruction by crating your dog or limiting their space is also advisable.

7. In addition to physical exercise there is also mental exercise. Both are tiring. Giving your dog an obedience lesson before you leave will also help to tire them. When a dog's personal needs are fulfilled they will be better behaved.

A five- to ten-minute obedience lesson, polishing some aspect of an exercise your dog is learning or has learned, really fulfills your dog's need for receiving your individual attention for appropriate behavior. Plus you will fill its soul with the message that it is a good dog. Self-fulfilling prophecy at work!

8. Your dog may have learned that when you pick up your keys or when you put on shoes it is a signal that you are leaving. If you have noticed that your dog is showing signs of distress at these times, you may want to do some counter-conditioning. Counter-conditioning means that you make new associations by giving the same

signals and pairing them with a wonderful dog treat. You could begin practicing this several times each day but, of course, not go anywhere.

C. When we are gone

Dog Owners Need to Behave When They Are Gone, Too!

The more time a person spends with their dog, the more badly behaved the person may be when they are without their dog. By badly behaved I mean they are constantly thinking about their dog and worrying about their dog being home alone. This behavior on the owner's part is a display of Separation Anxiety. I believe it is bad for both the owner and the dog because the owner's anxiousness can felt by the dog at a distance thus contributing to the dog's anxiousness at home.

D. When we first return home from being gone

Both your leaving and returning should be authentic, yet toned down. When you have to leave you have to leave, it's just a fact. And when you come home, of course you should be happy to see your dog, but you don't want to carry on and on about how much you missed them, even if that is how you feel. Avoid bringing a lot of emotion to these moments.

What if your dog was destructive when you were gone?

YOU SHOULD NOT SCOLD IN THE
AFTERMATH - EVER

Here are some rules to follow when and if you come home to a mess.

1. No scolding in the aftermath.
2. Never let the dog watch you clean up a mess. Put the dog outside or somewhere else when you clean up.
3. <u>Never Stay Mad</u>. Once you have cleaned up a mess and let your dog back inside, it's important to forgive and forget. After all, it's the behavior you dislike, not your dog. You don't want your dog to think you dislike them!
4. **Avoid giving your dog the opportunity to make the same mistake the next time you leave.**

E. Overnight
There is no right or wrong way for managing where your dog sleeps overnight. Every home is different, every dog is different, and every dog owner has its own unique needs. One parameter that has been established is that too much of any one thing is not good. What environment do you need to use to give your dog variety in where it spends its time? What environment encourages being together or encourages being independent? The answer to these questions depends on what went on during the rest of the day.

If you're someone who works a lot and is *almost never home*, then your dog needs to feel included in your life and overnight is a wonderful opportunity to do that. On the other hand, if you are home most of the time then sleeping arrangements that are more independent of you may make more sense.

Remember Maria and her dapple Dachshund named Duke? Well I'm glad to tell you that Duke has made huge progress, becoming more independent at last and he is also a happier dog. Maria used many of the exercises we discussed here, including tethering Duke on his spot and letting him experience her leaving the room and returning repeatedly when she was home. He receives lots of rewards, including food and praise and he finally understands that he has another choice in how to behave. His new experience has taught him she will return and he has learned how to accept that.

We all learn from our mistakes, but new behavior is built on our successes.

I briefly touched on the value of leaving and returning in this segment but you will want to read more about it in Section 2 Why Is Your Dog Destructive When You're Gone? **(Page 134 The Leaving and Returning Exercise Done Right!)**.

Oh, and let's not forget Lace, the white Labrador that I also mentioned in the beginning. She's doing great as well but she required a completely different strategy because her behavior was destructive. Different Strokes for Different Dogs! And more strategies ahead!

Managing Containment Phobia

The great news is that managing Containment Phobia may be easier than you'd ever anticipated. As a matter of fact, it may only take you as long as it takes you to make changes to the environment.

More good news:

a. Containment Phobia is not about you the owner. There's nothing you did wrong and there's nothing wrong with your dog. Your dog just needs its home environment set up differently.
b. Obedience training offers huge benefits, but all of the obedience training in the world is not going to resolve this issue.
c. Containment Phobic dogs are fabulous dogs! This is very likely the one and only issue you have ever had and ever will have with your dog, and it's fixable.

With that being said, there are numerous variables that can complicate matters. They are:

a. When the dog has been suffering with Containment Phobia for a long period of time (i.e., years) it has developed habits. Habits of panicking and/ or habits of destructive behavior may take longer for the dog to recover from. Strong longtime habits also increase the likelihood of regression because the dog has behaved that way for so long.
b. There will be a dollar investment in modifying the environment. Usually the dollar investment

is minimal compared to the investment you have already made in repairs.

c. A dog with a very mild level of Containment Phobia, teetering more on the diagnosis of Claustrophobia, may be able to dwell inside of a large home or an apartment as long as no one tries to shut the dog up in a small area. However, a moderate to high level of Containment Phobia is going to require a house with a fenced yard and a dog door. Not good news if the owner is currently living in an apartment.

d. It may be more difficult to take long trips with a dog that suffers from Containment Phobia. For example, leaving this dog in a hotel room without you will not be an option. Nor will it be an option to leave this dog in someone's yard that you're staying with while you go out to dinner. Solutions to these issues would need to be planned out in advance, but there are always solutions.

e. Boarding a dog with Containment Phobia in a regular kennel facility is not likely an option either. Other arrangements may need to be made here as well.

f. Leaving this dog in a car when you go inside somewhere may or may not be an issue. There are Containment Phobic dogs that love hanging out in cars and there are those that do not. If you have a dog that does not, it can be very expensive!

Over the years I have met a number of dog owners who come into my training facility expecting to have to go through some long-term training program because they think their dog has an extreme psychological case of Separation Anxiety. They are delighted and amazed to learn how simple the solutions may be.

Client Testimonial

"My dog is now 7 years old and finally, I learned the truth about her!"

I scheduled a private lesson at Garvin's Dog Training because, as I told them over the phone, my dog has Separation Anxiety. Ever since my dog was a puppy, she has destroyed window coverings at each home we moved to. Since this only occurred when we were gone, all the experts I talked to and the literature I read called it Separation Anxiety. There was very little that I could do about it since my wife and I had to go to work. We loved our dog and just hung in there. Typically, after several months of living at a new place, she seemed to settle in and the destruction would end; but, if we dared to move, it started all over again. Recently, I needed her to stay at my mother's house and sure enough, she destroyed my mother's window coverings as well. That's when I called Garvin's Dog Training.

It only took Karyn a few minutes to tell me it wasn't Separation Anxiety, but rather, a symptom of Containment Phobia. My dog had a fear of being trapped. The reason she only destroyed the window coverings was because her destruction was in relationship to trying to escape. Karyn proceeded to tell me that if Roxy had a dog door that would allow her the freedom to go outside and come inside when she wanted to, the destruction to the window coverings would end.

It only took me a moment to put two and two together and know that what she was saying was true. With the Separation Anxiety diagnosis, I had thought Roxy was destroying window coverings because she was at the window looking for me. There was nothing I could do to change that. Then I suddenly remembered how, at the last house she destroyed, we had put in a dog door for our senior dog that had bladder control issues, and sure enough, all of Roxy's destructive behavior stopped immediately. I still can't believe it. After all the money we wasted and all the destruction we incurred, all we needed was a dog door. I'm glad Garvin's knows what they're talking about since none of the other 'experts' did!

Modifying the Environment Therapy

The environment must be modified, because it is the environment that is triggering Containment Phobia in the dog. That is great news! When a dog suffers from Thunderstorm Phobia you cannot control the weather, but with Containment Phobia, the environment can be controlled and drugs are not necessary.

Every situation is unique and the solutions will vary from one home to the next, **however in all cases, the remedy is twofold:**

First, give the dog freedom of movement.

Second, have consequences in place to deter escape behavior.

It is also EXTREMELY important that these steps occur <u>simultaneously</u>.

First: Giving the Dog Freedom of Movement

Containment Phobic dogs need to be given the ability to move from one environment to the next and back again when it chooses. Freedom of movement from indoors to outdoors is the ideal solution. (In very mild cases, this is not always necessary.) In most homes this can be achieved by installing a dog door **and teaching** the dog how to use it. Containment Phobic dogs are usually very quick to learn to use a dog door, quicker than most! You must be convinced that your dog knows how to use its new door so that when it starts to panic, it makes the right choice.

A good way to see if this is an ideal solution for you and your dog is to leave your door open and try some test runs of leaving and returning, building up the time to at least a half an hour. If your dog is successful with this test then you can install your own dog door. (See Page 134 The Leaving and Returning Exercise Done Right!)

For questions about dog doors and to see what kinds of options there are available I would recommend **www.TucsonDogDoors.com**.

Giving your Dog Freedom of Movement May Present Other Concerns:

There may be additional reasons why you have not given your dog its freedom, and those concerns must be addressed now as well. Working one-on-one with a dog trainer/ behaviorist may offer you tremendous support as you go through this process. I would recommend going to **www.CanineProfessionals.com** to find a trainer in your area. (It's also a good idea to view their Google reviews before you contact them.) Another great referral source for a dog trainer may be your veterinarian.

Destructive Chewing

One of the most common concerns for dog owners who are considering giving their Containment Phobic dog free run is the fear of additional, destructive chewing.

There are several ways to address this:

a. Remove opportunities by dog / puppy proofing your house.

b. Spray items you know your dog would be attracted to with Grannicks Bitter Apple.

c. Installing an indoor, pet avoidance system.

d. Muzzle your dog. Leaving a dog with a muzzle on in your absence can be done safely. First you would select a muzzle which is large enough to allow your dog to drink and pant freely but is still a deterrent / safety net against destructive chewing. **Next, you must allow your dog to wear the muzzle in your presence for hours to be sure you feel safe with this measure before you would ever leave them home alone.** To first desensitize the dog, I recommend letting the dog wear the muzzle overnight, while asleep. The idea here is that the dog learns that when the muzzle goes on, it's time to just rest.

Client Testimonial

Our Basenji dog Che, has Containment Phobia. When we first started seeing Karyn for help with Che our first concern was how he screamed in his crate. It was making car rides, as well as life at home, almost unbearable. Her solution was simple ... quit using the crate! As a matter of fact, Karyn was the first professional to give us permission and to encourage us to not use the crate for Che.

However we had another problem that was his propensity towards destructive chewing while our backs were turned, both in the house and in our car. She urged us to use a muzzle selectively, so we did. It was great! We only use it for a period of anywhere from a few minutes to a couple of hours, and chewing is virtually a thing of the past. He was a bit resentful at first, but has now largely become comfortable with it.

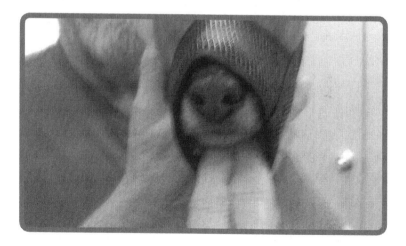

Leaving a muzzle on during the owner's absence can be done safely!

Soiling In the House

Soiling in the house is seldom an issue with Containment Phobic dogs as they are more than happy to go outside to eliminate. But while we are on the subject I wanted to share another solution that was necessary for Guiellermo.

Guiellermo was rescued by one of my clients after they found him running on the streets of Tucson. He had a number of behavior issues, but the most pressing was his Claustrophobic reaction when he was put in a crate in order to manage his behavior of marking indoors. (Marking is when a male dog urinates to mark his territory).

Guiellermo wore a diaper when he had freedom in the house. This was a perfect management tool that his owners chose to use when they were at home as well as when they were away. However, as we have already discussed, using any tool excessively will have negative effects. It was agreed that we needed another management solution besides diapers for Guiellermo for overnight. The solution was removing the crate door, but having him tethered so he had to remain in the crate. It worked!!!

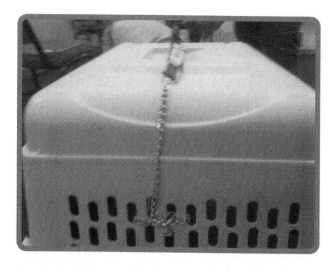

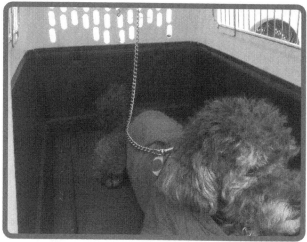

We chose a chain leash as Guiellermo was a master of chewing through leashes. The chain leash was then attached to the handle of the crate on the top and adjusted so that it was just the right length for Guiellermo. It came down from the top and was connected to his harness, which in this picture is underneath his little jacket. We were being careful to see that the leash was not of a length where it would get tangled under his feet. Guiellermo needed to be contained to prevent him from urinating without his diaper on. His crate was placed right next to his owner's bed, **when they could be with him and supervise him overnight.** This solution worked for them!

Excessive Barking

I understand that one of the reasons why you may not have given your dog access to outside could be that you're concerned about barking when you're not at home. A bark collar is an excellent way to manage barking in your absence. In my opinion the best bark collar available is the Garmin Bark Collar.

Second: Consequences to Deter Escape Behavior

You will also likely need to consider working with a professional in the pet containment industry in your area. Just type "Pet Containment" and your city's name into your internet search engine to find dealers in your area.

When a Containment Phobic dog panics and goes to the door, the window or a fence, it does so with the intent to use whatever force is necessary to bypass it. The dog is seeking the reward of escaping at these locations even when doing so may cause it physical harm. A dog with moderate to high levels of Containment Phobia needs to encounter a consequence in association with escape attempts. It must be a safe consequence of substantial force so that the dog will decide: "Oops! This is no longer an option." The consequence has to work when you're not around, which is why the electronic pet containment and pet avoidance solutions are ideal. In this circumstance, using electronic training equipment is truly in the dog's best interest and for their higher good.

The beauty of electronic correction is that it is safe and effective. The dog soon learns that everywhere is safe except for those places where it once tried to exit. It has a sense of freedom, and is also rewarded for making the right choice by avoiding punishing outcomes. And these training solutions work when you're not home!

There are both indoor and outdoor solutions that can combat all canine escape artists' tactics. You are the best one to decide whether you want to work with a particular company to install a system or if you want to purchase a do-it-yourself, owner installed system online.

Being the previous owner of a pet containment dealership, I can tell you firsthand that there are huge advantages to working with a reliable dealership.

1. They install the product and guarantee the equipment and the results.
2. They offer higher quality electronic equipment than you may be able to purchase online. When a dog is panicked and its adrenaline is flowing it may need a higher level of correction to get its attention and to be deterred from trying to escape. Professional equipment has variable levels of correction that will also offer higher levels of correction than you can usually purchase online. The company will help you find the right levels of correction for your dog.
3. They will also help you with the training process, **which is as important** as the equipment itself.

The pet containment solution offers consistency and, with owners receiving proper instruction, it minimizes the likelihood of human error.

Next let's address the list of escape behaviors that were mentioned early in Part I of this book. I will go through each item and suggest solutions for you to consider.

Escape Behaviors:

Escape Behavior: The ability to open doors with lever door handles.

Solution: Install knobs instead of lever door handles.

Escape Behavior: Ongoing attempts to break out of a dog crate.

Solution: Quit using the crate.

Escape Behavior: Ongoing attempts to escape kennel runs.

Solution: Quit using kennel runs.

Escape Behavior: Jumping over or going through dog gates.

Solutions:
a. Use a ScatMat® in conjunction with the dog gate. A ScatMat® is a vinyl mat which is battery operated. It gives off a safe static shock when touched. In this case it could be either draped over the dog gate or you could choose to lay it on the floor in front of the gate. The ScatMat® is designed for indoor use only. **www.DogTrainingEquipment.com**
b. Use an indoor pet avoidance system to create areas for the dog to avoid instead.

Escape Behavior: Jumping over fence.

Solutions:
a. Install a dog door so that the dog has an alternative; it can go inside.
b. Install an outdoor pet containment system.

c. Install an electric fence. An electric fence is visible to the dog. It consists of a wire running along the fence as a deterrent. The wire itself is electrified as opposed to the wire of a pet containment system that acts more like an antenna sending a signal to a collar. With the electric fence there is no special collar. The wire itself does all of the work. There are advantages and disadvantages to both systems, so you will need to decide for yourself what makes the most sense. I recommend the Red Snap'r brand electric fence: **www.RedSnapr.com**

Warning: With an electric fence you have one chance to do it right. If you hang this wire at the top of the fence the dog will likely go right over it. It's best to put the wire at the dog's nose height. Let it first walk up and sniff it with its moist nose. Hanging some ribbons on the wire will also make the wire more visible to the dog. **Another concern may be that other family dogs and children will also be exposed.**

Escape Behavior: Digging out underneath a fence.

Solutions:

a. Install a dog door so that the dog has an alternative, they can go inside.

b. Create a permanent physical barrier by pouring concrete or burying pavers along the fence.

c. Install an outdoor pet containment system.

d. Install an electric fence.

Escape Behavior: Chewing and digging through a fence.

Solutions:
a. Install a dog door so that the dog has an alternative, they can go inside.
b. Install an outdoor pet containment system.
c. Install an electric fence.

Escape Behavior: Chewing and digging through interior walls.

Solution:
a. Install a dog door so that the dog has an alternative, they can go outside.
b. Install an indoor pet avoidance system.
c. ScatMat®

Escape Behavior: Destroying exits when contained in a room. This could include doors, windows, window coverings such as curtains blinds, etc.

Solution: Don't shut this dog in a room!

Escape Behavior: Breaking through glass windows.

Solution:
a. Install a dog door so that the dog has an alternative and can go outside.
b. Install an indoor pet avoidance system.

Escape Behavior: When sufficiently contained in the back yard, destroying the house trying to get inside.

Solution: Install a dog door to allow dog to get in and out freely.

Never Depend on a Remote
Electronic Training Collar for Escape Behavior

For higher levels of Containment Phobia where the electronic consequence is part of the solution, the owner should never depend on the remote electronic training collar. The remote collar was never designed to be a solution for escape behavior. A remote training collar is owner operated. The dog owner has to be there to provide the consequence. Because this behavior is innate, the dog will test the exits from time to time. Once it discovers there is no longer a consequence in place, because the owner will not always be there, it will likely regress and escape.

The Only Other Solution Is to Never Leave
Your Dog Home Alone.

I would be remiss if I forgot to mention that you also want to MICROCHIP your dog.

The Containment Phobic dog should be wearing a collar with tags at all times. Accidents do happen! Microchipping your dog is the best back-up plan you could possibly have.

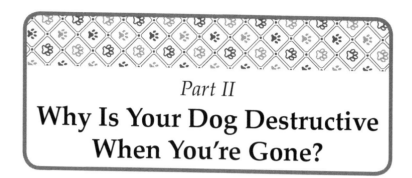

Part II

Why Is Your Dog Destructive When You're Gone?

The Behavior Management Equation

The Behavior Management Equation is a formula for dog owners to use whenever they are looking to resolve a behavioral issue with their dog. In fact there are **only** 3 components to this equation that need to be taken into consideration.

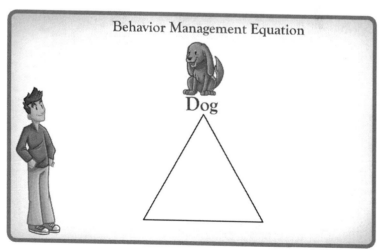

Behavior Management Equation

Dog

#1. The Dog

The first factor that has to be taken into consideration is **the dog**. Fortunately, most people are committed to keeping their dog. As a matter of fact, I'm sure that you are one of those people or you wouldn't be taking the time to read this book. I thank you for being that kind of person.

We take care of things we love. It's actually in the taking care of, and seeing our way through tough times, that we deepen our appreciation for what we have. Deepening our appreciation only strengthens our commitment and our ability to love unconditionally. That's that then, we are keeping the dog!

Desire

#2. The Dog Has a Desire: a reason why it behaves this way.

DOES "WHY" EVEN MATTER?

In most cases why a dog behaves the way it does matters very much. Understanding "why" can actually help us to eliminate the cause, as in cases of Containment Phobia. Eliminating the cause can also eliminate the effect, the destructive behavior.

In other cases understanding "why" may not help us eliminate the desire, but at least we understand what action we must take to get the situation under control. For example, why did the dog break into the kitchen trash? Most commonly they do this because they want to add variety to their diet. It's a scavenger hunt for dogs that proves to be very rewarding. Even when there is no food in the trash, the dog may have learned that the hunt itself is still fun. Breaking into the trash may have become a habit. But once again, knowing "why" does not help me to change the dog's desire, nor does it help me resolve the issue of the dog breaking into the trash.

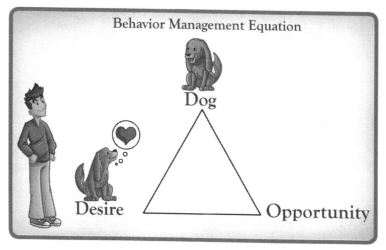

Behavior Management Equation

Dog

Desire

Opportunity

#3. Opportunity

But I can stop giving the dog the opportunity to get into the trash. Here is where we have to step up and manage the situation differently. I don't want to argue with Mother Nature; I know I will lose. In this particular case I am not going to be able to modify the dog's desire to get in the trash completely. I could and should listen to my dog's behavior and start adding more variety to its daily meals but even then ... when I'm gone I need to quit giving this dog the opportunity. I just need to put the trash up ... period.

When we are confronted with a situation we cannot change, we are challenged to change ourselves.

Viktor Frankl

In this book I have broken down the reasons why dogs are destructive during their owners' absence into six categories. We have already discussed the first three, Separation Anxiety, Claustrophobia and Containment Phobia.

The remaining three are:

- The Psychological Approach: Frustrating Factors for Dogs
- Mismanagement
- Thunderstorm Phobia

In this next section, the Psychological Approach we will take an in-depth look at

Answering the Additional Big "Whys?"

Frustrating Factors for Dogs:

Dogs have problems and feel frustrations similarly to the way we do. When a person is unhappy he/she can vent frustrations in an untold number of ways: by overeating, drinking too much, doing drugs, getting depressed and staying depressed or going shopping, just to name a few. But one thing is for sure, whatever we choose to do out of frustration, we will likely do it in excess of what is good for us. A dog, on the other hand, is limited to expressing its frustrations through one of its innate behaviors such as chewing, digging, barking and soiling in the house. **Whichever behavior a dog chooses, when it does it in excess, it is a sign of the dog's frustration.**

The Psychological Approach

I was first introduced to a list of frustrating factors for dogs in the book <u>Behavior Problems in Dogs</u> by William E. Campbell (Mosby Year Book, Inc., 1975). I have always been grateful to Bill Campbell for his insight and the direction I received by following the original list he created. The following list has proven to be tried and true in my own practice since 1977.

Though William E. Campbell is no longer with us, he will always be remembered. He is also remembered in the International Association of Canine Professionals Hall of Fame (IACP). The following list is based on his original list along with some modifications made by myself. Permission to use this list was granted by Peggy Campbell, 2015.

Is Your Dog As Frustrated As You Are?

I would like you to go through the following list and check off all the frustrating factors that you think accurately describe your situation. Typically, the more items you check, the more frustrated your dog is and the more it **acts out** as well. After you go through the list, I will give you my interpretation of what each factor means, as well as possible solutions or remedies.

- Owner's leadership not established
- Emotional homecomings and/or departures
- Separation anxiety
- Isolation, especially during the critical socialization period from 5 to 12 weeks of age
- Isolation as a form of punishment
- Restrictions of freedom
- Psychological trauma associated with a place or situation
- Physical abuse as a means of punishment
- Scolding in the aftermath
- Emotional stress of owner, even when stress is unrelated to the dog
- Owner's dislike of dog
- Change of routine / habit factors
- Any big change of environment such as relocating or owners leaving on a vacation
- Boredom
- Physiological problems and/or illness (including teething)
- Extreme weather conditions
- Lack of proper exercise

Owner's Leadership Not Established

Solution: Obedience training

When you train your dog, you strengthen your role as the leader. Your dog learns that it can look to you for direction. It begins to understand that you have something to teach him, that you expect something from him, and that you expect him to succeed. Great teaching skills give you great leadership qualities. This is very reassuring to a dog.

Obedience commands can be the tools you use to tell your dog what to do instead of doing it for him. For example, you tell him to STAY rather than holding him back from running out the door. You tell him to SIT rather than grabbing him so that he can't jump on someone. Remember, all the "NOs" in the world won't tell a dog what you want. "NO" only communicates what you don't want. Redirecting your dog acknowledges his intelligence and helps you to **earn your leadership.**

Leadership is Something We Have to Earn
Contrary to Popular Belief, We Are Not Entitled

An owner may say, "We don't need obedience training, he does everything I ask; the dog is perfect except for this one problem." Obedience training can make a difference, even in this case, because the dog may have learned to take your praise and affection for granted. You're so pleased with him that he doesn't have to try to please you anymore. Your reaction to his misbehaving actually becomes more rewarding. Obedience training emphasizes the fact that the dog has a job and responsibilities. He has to be a good dog for your praise. If this sounds like your situation, you may start by having your dog do things such as sit before you pet him.

Another owner may reveal that they seem to be constantly correcting their dog for one thing or another. The dog is continuously acting out. This owner really *needs* to put their dog into training to be able to reward their dog with well earned attention instead.

There are dogs so accustomed to an owner's negative attention they are desensitized to it and find it rewarding. Wesley C. Becker, in Parents are Teachers, refers to this as "The Criticism Trap." Becker used the grumpy old school teacher as an example: The grumpy old school teacher turns her back on the class to write on the chalkboard and instantly the kids are standing up or acting out. The teacher turns around and yells, "Sit down!" The kids sit down and so the teacher is rewarded for yelling, "Sit down," but as soon as she turns her back again, the students are standing up again. Why? To get her to yell: "Sit down!" **That's the trap. We yell "NO," the dog quits and we're rewarded, but then the dog does it again to get us to yell "NO!" Negative attention can be very rewarding.**

Obedience training is an opportunity for you to reward your dog for being good. It can motivate him to want to be good. **I've always said that a dog that knows he's good usually doesn't want to do bad things.** A person who values honesty wouldn't tell a lie because he or she values the goodness of honesty. Well behaved dogs have also learned to value rewards.

Emotional Homecomings and/or Departures

The owner who lectures his dog before leaving the house may be making the situation worse. There is a self-fulfilling prophecy that states that what you expect is what you get. "You be a good boy now and don't chew anything up!" We who believe in a dog's sixth sense will tell you that the dog may actually receive the visualization you're sending of his chewing and take it as a command.

Nor is it a good idea to share feelings of sadness. The owner, who is sad about leaving and shares these feelings, leaves the dog depressed. A depressed dog may also act out.

Dogs are innately joyful upon their owner's return home. It's only natural that the dog's owner should express joy upon seeing the dog as well. It is also wise to bring calm energy and discipline to this moment. The owner may want to be cautious about rewarding over-the-top, overjoyed habits of greeting people.

Solution: Your leaving and returning should not be a huge deal. You should not lecture your dog before going out or upon returning home.

Separation Anxiety

Many social animals are distressed when separated from their companions or loved ones. Feelings of loss are a result of love and attachment. It is not uncommon for a child to throw a tantrum when left with a baby-sitter or for an adult to feel depressed when his/her spouse takes a trip. Dogs are by nature social so they are more likely to show distress when left alone. Emotional attachment is especially important for animals whose survival is dependent on group living. We've all heard the phrase, "dogs are pack animals." While many dogs feel some level of frustration when left alone, certain dogs express it by various behaviors such as chewing, soiling in the house, howling, barking, and marking.

Solution: You can't always change what frustrates your dog, but you can anticipate it and control the environment.

If your dog follows you everywhere when you are home, you could try to create some ways to distance yourself so that he won't be so upset when you leave. You could, for example, have your dog lie down and stay on its bed while you go out of sight for brief periods. You can teach him to be more independent by not allowing him to be constantly in your lap or at your feet.

Your dog may have also learned that when you pick up your keys or put on your shoes, these are signals that you are leaving. If you have noticed that your dog is showing signs of distress at these times, you may want to do some counter-conditioning. Counter-conditioning means that you make new associations by giving the same signals, but pairing them with a wonderful dog treat. You could begin practicing this several times each day, but not go anywhere.

Most dogs become frustrated and express their frustrations in the first 30 minutes after the owner leaves. Retraining would involve leaving for brief interval periods of time, such as 5 minutes, 10 minutes, then 5 minutes, then 8 minutes, then 15 minutes and so on, working your way up to 45 minutes and one hour without incident. Your dog will become accustomed to these short trips and learn from experience that you are coming back. When you can leave for 45 minutes to one hour without a problem, you have made substantial progress.

None of these suggestions by themselves is a cure all. I would suggest you work at this from every direction.

Isolation, Especially During Critical Socialization Periods from 5 to 12 Weeks of Age

When a puppy is removed either from its mother or its littermates at an unnaturally early time, it will be deprived from learning critical socialization skills. Another example could be a puppy that was raised in a kennel situation where it was isolated from everything including people. This puppy, as a result, may grow up to be fearful of everyone and everything - an unhappy way to live.

Solution: If your dog is fearful, or lacking in normal socialization skills it is never too late to relearn and rebuild their confidence. A true leader and teacher will help him to face his fears and overcome them. Unfortunately, many people want to avoid any conflicts because they believe it is the kind thing to do. This only compounds the problem. You can either choose to support your dog so he becomes more confident or you can avoid conflicts ultimately causing your dog to continue to be fearful. If you choose to help him become more confident, you can start by making a list of all the things that frighten him and begin counter-conditioning. You may want to enlist the services of a dog trainer. This type of healing will produce a happier, better behaved dog.

Isolation as a Form of Punishment

I know that "time out" works with children, but as a form of punishment for dogs it is not recommended. While isolation can be a punitive measure, it does not teach the dog how to behave. As a result, at some point, the dog will have to be isolated again.

Punishing a dog by isolating it in the crate could also teach it to resent its crate.

Solution: If you are tempted to isolate your dog because he is misbehaving, you might first stop and ask yourself what you want him to do instead. Think more in terms of teaching the dog what to do. We all learn more from our successes.

Restrictions of Freedom

This usually refers to dogs that are **confined too much or dogs that are suffering from "cabin fever."**

It could be that the owner has overused the crate or other confinement techniques. It also could be that the owner thinks a yard is all the freedom a dog needs. If you live on a property of several acres or on a farm or ranch, your dog probably has a wonderful life outdoors. However, in urban areas most yards just aren't big enough. A scale for comparison would be the wolf in the wild that is estimated to travel as much as 90 miles per day.

Solution: Dogs need exercise and change. They need to be in the house as well as be able to go outside, go for walks and car rides. They need freedom and variety. A worldly dog is usually much more stable.

A Change Is as Good as a Break

Psychological Trauma Associated with a Place or Situation

These dogs have learned to be fearful of certain stimuli. They feel out of control and panic in certain situations.

Car sickness is probably the most common example of this. Most car sickness is a result of psychological trauma rather than motion sickness. A puppy could associate the car and a car ride with the pain of Separation Anxiety from when it was removed from its first home and littermates.

Solution: Ask the breeder or foster parent to take the puppy for some fun rides before you bring it to its new home. And once you get your puppy, continue to take it for fun rides early on, rather than only taking trips to the veterinary clinic, for an example.

In addition, no matter what fear your dog has learned, you can help him to relearn by providing new experiences. You can have a more confident and secure animal with less frustrations. You may also want to enlist a dog trainer to help facilitate you through the process.

Physical Abuse as a Means of Punishment

Physical abuse is what I would refer to as an **undisciplined discipline**. The premise for a person behaving in a physically abusive way is always displaced anger. Being abusive is being undisciplined. Disciplined discipline is based on love. It requires thoughtfulness and is intended for everyone's highest good.

Beating a dog is never acceptable. It will not work and it will also cause additional problems that you do not want.

Certain dogs may become submissive and insecure from being hit. A submissive dog could have problem behaviors such as cowering, submissive wetting or excessive barking. It may learn to displace frustration through inappropriate aggression as well. These are not behaviors you want in your dog.

Physical abuse will not allow a healthy rewarding relationship to develop. Nor will it teach the dog a correct way to behave. The dog will only want to escape and avoid the person who abuses him as opposed to being open and receptive to learning.

Solution: The abuser needs to learn How to Manage Their Temper! Learning to manage their anger will help this person in all of their relationships for the rest of their life. It is NOT OK to act abusive, ever! Practicing anger management skills with the dog is just the beginning. We all have to work at becoming the person we want to be. Our dogs can help us become better people and they will always give us a second chance.

If you catch your dog in the act of doing something wrong, there is certainly nothing wrong with punishment. A good scolding, for example, may help the dog change his mind about the pleasures of misbehaving. It is important that an effective correction be followed with redirection, showing the dog what he should do instead. It is also important to reassure your dog within 10 or 15 minutes that you love him. The dog has to know that it was the behavior, not him that you disliked.

Scolding in the Aftermath
First of all, we need to keep things in perspective. A dog has no idea of the kind of financial damage it is doing when it destroys property. Nor do they understand how much work it is for us to clean up

a mess or why even cleaning up a mess is important. They are as clueless in this regard as a two- or three-year -old child who finds a can of spray paint and sprays daddy's car a new color. Keeping this in perspective helps us to manage our temper and disappointment.

The "aftermath" means that more than three minutes have elapsed since the incident and you're finding it. When it has been more than 3 or 4 minutes, it's too late for a scolding.

The dog is only able to live in the present and be in the moment. Human beings on the other hand are fully aware of not only the present, but the past and the future. It quite naturally makes sense to us that the dog **should** be able to understand in the aftermath, but the dog will make different associations.

If you search the house as soon as you get home and find that the dog destroyed something and scold him, he just learns that you come home, look around and then get mad! It doesn't make sense to the dog. The same thing is true with giving the dog a cookie if you didn't find a mess. Your dog is making different associations.

Scolding in the aftermath can actually create the circumstances you're trying to eliminate. Dogs have a biological clock that tells them it's about time for you to arrive home. If you frequently come home and get angry, your dog could get in a habit of expecting this. The anticipation of your angry arrival may actually be causing the issue you're having. Often a dog exhibits frustrated behavior either right after the owner leaves or **just before they get home.** Scolding in the aftermath contributes to the **"just before the owner gets home"** group.

Dogs do learn from experience. I have heard people say, "I know he knows he has done something wrong because when I come home and find he has destroyed something, he is cowering or hiding." But thinking back, haven't there also been times when you have come home and he's acted as if he had done something wrong, yet you couldn't find anything anywhere? This would be evidence of what I'm suggesting is true, that this dog is just learning to associate that when you first get home you get really, really upset!

Other people say, "I know he knows he has done something wrong because I just point to it and he takes off." This is because he has learned what you look like and how you behave before you get angry. Dogs are masters at reading body language.

Scolding in the aftermath does not work for the vast majority of dogs. The only association a dog may make is that a mess in your presence means trouble. He still won't associate punishment or anything negative with the act of doing it unless you actually catch him in the act.

Solution: It is most effective to scold or punish a dog when you catch him in the act. Never say or do anything if it been longer than three minutes since the incident occurred.

Emotional Stress of Owner, Even When Stress Is Unrelated to the Dog

Dogs are sensitive to their owners. I can think of many examples of how amazingly sensitive they are. One of my favorites is the service dog who can actually notify his owner who is about to have an epileptic seizure, which gives the owner time to lie down in a safe position. Is there any doubt that dogs are sensitive to our moods? I have gone to homes on numerous occasions where the owner was totally puzzled as to why his/her adult dog, that had never been a problem, was suddenly doing terrible things. They would exclaim, "As if life isn't bad enough! Frank died a month ago, I lost my job and now this - even the dog has gone sour." The owner doesn't realize that the dog is misbehaving solely because it is stressed because its owner is under so much stress.

Solution: Do you remember the routine you had with your dog when life wasn't so stressful? It will be good therapy for both of you to resume that routine. Let your dog do his job of cheering you up.

Owner's Dislike of Dog

Dogs are sensitive and not easily fooled. They can feel when the owner dislikes them. No sense in denying this one if you have gotten yourself in a rut.

Many people begin to dislike their dog because they believe that their dog is spiteful. The owner will say, "I know he's just being spiteful; he was mad when I left." Dogs are not spiteful creatures. If I have learned anything from dogs, it's the true meaning of unconditional love. I'm sure you have heard, DOG spelled forwards or backwards is unconditional love. Yes, your dog was upset and yes, that's what contributed to the behavior, but no, he did not do it to get back at you.

Solution: It is important to understand the difference between not liking a dog as opposed to not liking its behavior. It is fruitless to stay angry for long periods of time and rehearse your anger.

If the Grass Is Always Greener on the Other Side, It May Be Getting More Water!!!

If you feel your relationship has been damaged, you need to be the one to go out of your way to change things with your dog.

One of my favorite exercises for dog owners that are trying to get back on the right path with their dog is to have them make a list of 10 things they love about their dog. Just 10 things! Once the list is made, the key is to read the list each day and feel each of the items on the list. People learn from experience too. We need to experience liking and loving once again. Give this exercise one week of sincere effort and you will be amazed!

Change of Routine / Habit Factors

Routine in our lives gives us a sense of stability. It is frustrating when you suddenly can't do something that you routinely did each day. Most dogs find comfort in and rely on a routine.

Solution: First, it is important to avoid breaking the routine as much as possible. Second, you can compensate for a break in routine by substituting. For example, you can't go for that 20-minute walk before work, but you could play ball for five minutes. Third, if you have to change the routine and you know your dog will act out, you can avoid trouble by controlling the environment and reducing the opportunity for misbehavior.

Any Big Change in the Environment, Such as Relocating or Owners Leaving for Vacation

This can be a huge upset to a dog.

Solution: It is important to soften the blow any way you can.

If you anticipate trouble, you may also want to avoid giving your dog the opportunity to misbehave. I believe more dogs start new bad habits when their owners go on vacation than at any other time. Maybe the house sitter shouldn't give him the liberties or opportunities he has when you're at home. Then again, maybe a house sitter is a bad idea for this dog.

Boredom

The more intelligent the dog, the more easily bored it can become. It is usually the very intelligent dog that gets into trouble.

Solution: It is important to have routine rituals such as regular feeding times, walks, or indoor/outdoor times. The mental exercise of obedience training also can resolve some of the frustration of boredom that dogs feel. It gives you more ways to interact when you are together. And don't forget to get your dog out of the house. Cabin fever is one of the biggest causes for boredom.

Physiological Problems and/or Illness (including teething)

Just as teething influences behavior, so can a physical illness, infection, or disorder.

Solution: It is always a good idea to consult with your veterinarian and rule out the possibility of any physical problems that could be contributing to behavior issues.

Extreme Weather Conditions

The weather can affect the behavior of a dog. Thunderstorms can be emotionally traumatic for some dogs, and humidity can be physically painful for the arthritic dog. Difficult weather conditions may also affect the owner's ability to exercise their dog.

Solution: You may want to consult with your veterinarian regarding whether medications would be appropriate for your dog if their physical discomfort is weather related. You can't change the weather, but you can take preventive measures to make your dog as comfortable as possible. You can also consider a commercial dog day care if your dog is young and needing more indoor exercise.

Lack of Proper Exercise

All dogs require exercise. The requirements will vary according to the breed and age of the dog. When these requirements are not fulfilled, problems with behavior may result.

Solution: Exercise is an excellent preventative; it generally produces an overall happier dog. There is a wise saying that a tired dog is a good dog. Exercise doesn't always mean going for a walk. It could mean playing a game such as throwing a ball. It could mean taking a young dog to doggy daycare a couple of times each week or going to a dog park. If for some reason you can't personally exercise your dog, you can perhaps find someone to help. There are more supplemental dog services for dog owners today than ever before.

Mismanagement

The price for mismanagement is that the dog learns to find the destructive behavior, the act of destroying whatever it is destroying, fun and rewarding. The dog was either mismanaged growing up or it is being mismanaged now.

Mismanagement Almost Always Begins with Young Puppies

In the cartoon illustration for mismanagement, we see a young woman who is a slob with very few management skills. Not only does she **not manage** the orderliness of her own home, she has obviously **not managed this dog's behavior growing up.** She doesn't really care if he chews on the couch cushion, she thinks it's just an old couch and she wants to get a new one anyways.

Worse still, rather than accepting responsibility for the dog's inappropriate behaviors, she blames it on the dog having Separation Anxiety when nothing could be further from the truth. **The really scary thing is that these types of people exist.** When people do not understand that they need to accept responsibility for their dog's behavior, they look outside of themselves for things to change. Then, when they finally get tired of the situation, they make it someone else's problem and they dump the dog.

Fixing the Blame on the Dog Will Never Fix the Problem!

The story continues: After the dog is relinquished, a responsible caring person adopts the dog and now has to change the dog's habits and teach the dog new behaviors. Bless them!

I was called out on a new adoption recently. The dog was somewhere between three and four years of age and unfortunately I could tell right away that he had been raised by the type of person I just described. The new owner was under the misguided impression that the dog had Separation Anxiety because that's the diagnosis some experts had given her.

The new owner was exercising this dog like crazy and doing everything right. She told me how when she first left him at home, shortly after getting him, how he ripped into her sofa. He had actually pulled the couch around the room (the couch was on a tile floor) and then proceeded to take one bite out of each and every cushion. **Like a naughty teenager waiting for his parents to go on vacation, this dog couldn't wait for the owner to leave so that it could PARTY!!!**

Destructive Behavior Can Become a Habit – Simply Because It Is Fun!

When this dog's destructive behavior first began, whenever that was, it may have been as a result of a frustration or from growing up in an environment where the dog was mismanaged. Regardless, at this point in the dog's life, it's merely a habit that it enjoys engaging in. In which case, why the dog started the behavior initially really doesn't matter now. The bottom line is the behavior needs to STOP! **And the new dog owner needed to stop giving this dog the opportunity.**

Understanding Behavior, Having Realistic Expectations and Effective Management Techniques

All Behavior Is Either Innate or Learned

To best illustrate this I have listed a few examples for people as well as dogs.

PEOPLE		DOGS	
Learned	**Innate**	**Learned**	**Innate**
Driving Reading Writing	Talking Eating Breathing Sleeping Smiling Crying	Walk on lead Sit on command	Barking Eating Playing Chewing Digging Jumping

- A behavior can be both innate and learned at the same time. A dog's desire to chew is innate. However, if the dog has learned to target shoes, chewing shoes is learned.
- Innate behaviors are permanent. They are part of our Divine Nature and ensure survival in the world. And they are manageable.
- Learned behaviors are also manageable and can often be extinguished. We can prevent having shoes destroyed by:
  a. Managing the dog's **opportunity** to chew on shoes.

b. **Redirecting the desire** to chew towards items we find appropriate. **Developing new habits.**

c. Incorporating strategies using **consequences, which will punish** the dog's desire to engage in that activity in the future. This will then **encourage the dog to make different choices.** For example, the owner might deliberately make a shoe available that had been thoroughly sprayed with Grannick's Bitter Apple. After the puppy finds the shoe and also finds it repulsive, the owner would then remove the shoe until the next shoe avoidance training lesson.

The desire to chew and teethe is innate. However, what a dog learns to chew on is learned. Chewing on furniture and gutting cushions and pillows are learned behaviors!

Similarly, needing to potty is innate, but **where** the dog learns to eliminate is learned. It is our job to show good leadership, control the environment, and teach puppies as well as adult dogs that we expect appropriate behavior.

I may be showing my age here, but I will never forget my amazement when I first saw stuffed toys hanging in the dog toy aisle at a pet store. Stuffed toys with squeakers in them to boot! It was no surprise to me that dogs love stuffed toys. I had been helping dog owners teach their dogs to leave their children's stuffed toys alone for years. Can you imagine going into a pet store and finding an aisle with shoes hanging in it? That's how preposterous it seemed to me. I knew it could mean behavior issues, and it has.

Gutting Stuffed Toys Is Often the Gateway Behavior to Destroying Cushions and Furniture

Many dogs play nicely with stuffed toys - squeaking them, tossing them, retrieving them, **and that's fine.** They can be wonderful toys for some dogs. However, other dogs learn that it's fun to gut stuffed toys and take the squeakers out. Squeaker or no squeaker, **the act of gutting a stuffed toy is pulling the threads apart and pulling out the stuffing. Your furniture and cushions are oftentimes stuffed with the very same materials.**

Dogs usually learn to destroy pillows, cushions and furniture because:

a. As **teething puppies** they were given numerous plush toys to play with which they instead learned to love to gut and pull out the stuffing.

b. As **teething puppies** they were given **a dog bed in their crate** which they destroyed. And if that wasn't bad enough, the owners bought this same teething puppy another dog bed and **gave it the same opportunity** to do it a second time. The dog's owner mismanaged the situation which contributed to developing a bad habit.

c. As **teething puppies** they were left outdoors and **given the opportunity** to access, play with and destroy cushions off of furniture.

d. As **teething puppies** they were left unsupervised indoors for long periods of time and **given the opportunity** and access to furniture and cushions.

Realistic Expectations

Contrary to Popular Belief,

You CAN Lead a Horse to Water and Make It Drink

It is realistic to expect that you can and will be able to live harmoniously with your dog. Whether you are starting with a new puppy or you have adopted a dog from a shelter or a rescue group, you can make it work. What we know is that each dog and every puppy is a unique individual. What it will take to accomplish your goals with one dog may be very different from the next, but I assure you, you can make it work. There are many roads that lead to Rome and there are at least 100 different ways to wash dishes. You just have to discover what works for you with this particular dog/ puppy that you are training.

Having a strong belief system is important, as this will get you through the rough times. **You need to know that you can do this!**

> *Whatever you believe, you will be 100% correct.*
>
> *Harvey Firestone*

Learning is not instant! When one strategy fails, you have not failed, but rather you have just learned what didn't work. It's now time to try something else. **In this day and age, you have every tool imaginable available to you to help you train your dog.**

Effective Management Techniques
It is much easier for a dog to learn correct behavior from the beginning. The goal is to have your dog repeat behaviors you want early on and develop good habits.

For most people, their ultimate goal would be to have a dog that has freedom around the house and is trustworthy when they are home as well as when they are away.

If You Want a Dog To Be Trustworthy, You Need To Trust It

The Integrated Approach to dog training would recommend that you approach this from several directions:

- **Obedience training** helps you to develop your relationship and establish yourself as a teacher. You will also learn how to train your dog. Your dog/ puppy needs to know that they can look up to you for direction and that you are on their side. You believe in them, you expect them to be good and the best way to get your attention is by working with you. You're a team.

- **Fulfilling your dog's needs.** Once again because each dog is different, they all have different needs. Whether that is dietary, behavioral, physical, emotional or mental, it is in fulfilling their needs that our needs are fulfilled. Refer to the solutions you learned about earlier in the Psychological Approach (page 99).

- **Selecting the right training tools** or dog training equipment enables you to control the environment and obedience train your dog. If the tools you are using are not working, try something else. At DogTrainingEquipment.com there is a product information library to help you.

- **Controlling the environment** ensures that the behaviors you want can be repeated. You need to be able to manage and teach your dog the right habits that work for you and for your home environment.

**Remember, You Control the Environment &
Your Dog's Opportunities**

Getting back to the story of the woman who adopted an adult dog that already had the habit of targeting and destroying couches … poor thing! (The woman, I mean.) Trying to do everything right, she removed the first couch the dog destroyed and went without a couch in her sunroom. Once she removed the couch, things were better. The dog had a dog door, she was controlling how much access the dog had to the rest of the house, and as I said earlier, she was exercising him like crazy. He was well behaved during her absence. After some time had passed she got another couch that someone she knew was giving away. The very first time she left the dog alone with the new couch, he ripped into it again … taking one bite out of each and every cushion. She was devastated. She called me.

I always find these kinds of appointments a little awkward. The owner tells me that the dog has Separation Anxiety, that she's sure he's doing this because he's insecure because he's been re-homed, and basically the whole sad story of who-knows-what happened to him previously. She is expecting me to go into the psychological approach of possible reasons for why, as if that's the solution. I'm just looking at the remnants of this most recently destroyed couch and thinking this dog is simply badly behaved. I don't know how or why he learned to do this initially, but he is a master couch eater and is obviously having fun doing it now. This is one of those times where all of the "whys" and sob stories of what might have happened to him at previous homes will not fix the problem. "Why" does not matter in this instance. This dog has a great home now and the couch eating behavior needs to stop.

Let's take into consideration The Integrated Approaches mentioned earlier:

- **Obedience training**
- **Fulfilling your dog's needs**
- **Selecting the right training tools**
- **Controlling the environment**

Obedience Training: This particular owner was already great at giving the dog structure; she was a great leader and the dog did obey her commands. More obedience training was not going to stop this dog from destroying the couch.

Fulfilling your dog's needs: As far as fulfilling his needs, the owner did a great job in this area as well. It was hard for her to hear this because she wanted to think there was something wrong with him, some need that was not being fulfilled. I had to lay it on the line to help her see that she was doing everything right. She was fulfilling all of his needs and there was nothing that he was lacking. This was a bad behavior habit that he had learned somewhere else. It is no wonder he was relinquished to a shelter. Someone else didn't know how to manage this behavior either.

The solutions for her were in the areas of either: **selecting the right training tools and/or controlling the environment.**

If she was determined to have a couch in this area of her house, then we had to defend it.

The Right Training Tools:

For this particular dog, I felt that he was way too destructive to be deterred by Grannicks Bitter Apple Spray. Nor did I recommend a ScatMat® to keep him from jumping up on the couch because I was pretty sure he would destroy that as well. For training equipment options, I suggested:

1. Installing an indoor pet avoidance system in the area where the couch is. This electronic unit transmits a radio signal to the dog's collar to teach the dog to avoid the couch when she wasn't home. Rather than keeping the dog away from the couch, the dog could continue to have its freedom, but it would learn to avoid the couch. Ouch!

    Even though it was very important to her to give him his freedom, she didn't care for this idea. Nor did she want to consider the dollar investment for the training equipment as she was on a very tight budget.

Controlling the Environment:

2. Shutting him outside when she was gone. She had several reasons for why she didn't want to do that.

3. Crating him inside when she was gone. She already had a crate. She had several reasons for why she didn't want to do that either.

4. Learn to live without having a couch in this area. That made the most sense to her. We talked about how she could move things around and bring in more plants to fill the space and decorate the room. She finally got excited about the prospects for redesigning the room without a couch and she was happy.

The couch she and her family used for actually sitting on and watching TV was in a different room. That couch was safe because she could deny the dog's access to it by simply closing a door when she was gone. This was the solution for her situation. She now saw the situation for what it was, she had realistic expectations, and they can now live happily ever after.

Here are some more management techniques to consider in managing your dogs' behavior and teaching them to be trustworthy:

Overnight
Giving a dog free run of the house overnight is about as close as we can simulate to you being gone completely. Taking gradual steps in this direction is also a good way to test the dog's trustworthiness.

I frequently encourage dog owners to begin by allowing their dog to sleep in their bedroom overnight.

Your puppy/dog could be managed overnight in your room by:

Sleeping in a Crate

Crating your dog in your bedroom overnight can be a great way to manage the dog's behavior. **This is especially true if you do not need to rely on the crate for extended periods of time during the day.** In the beginning the crate door would be closed, and then after a period of time, usually 4 to 8 weeks or until the puppy is done teething, the crate door could begin being left open. When you first start leaving the door to the crate open, you might either close the bedroom door or block the dog's access to the rest of the house with a dog gate to limit its opportunities. Over the course of a few more weeks, the owner could expand the amount of area the dog has outside of the bedroom door overnight.

Sleeping Tethered next to Your Bed

Working in the same way crating does by minimizing the dog's space, it reduces the likelihood that your dog will soil in that area and it also reduces the dog's opportunity to chew on things. Tethering a dog next to your bed is a great alternative to crating. I would also recommend beginning with a chain leash so the puppy/dog never experiences chewing through a leash.

It's all about balance. Too much of anything is not good. In other words, if your puppy/dog needs to be crated for a substantial period of time during the day when you're gone, then tethering them next to your bed or in your bedroom is a great alternative for overnight.

Sleeping in Bed with You
Contrary to what you may think, I also have no problem with allowing a dog to sleep in bed with you. Quite honestly it's no one's business who you sleep with. Very young puppies may need to bond and they are not going to be able to make it all night without relieving themselves. Having your puppy or newly adopted dog in the room with you where you can hear them begin to stir and fuss is a great way to begin teaching them that if they need to be let out, they just need to make some noise and you will get up and let them out.

Note: For a really young puppy, let's say 8 weeks of age, you may want to consider putting them in a Sherpa bag and having it in the bed with you. This way you don't have to worry about rolling over on them, and they are definitely going to whine to wake you up if they need to go outside to potty. When this is their first experience with a crate of sorts it will also teach them to relax and go to sleep after they enter.

A lot of people are concerned with allowing a young puppy to sleep in their bed knowing that they will want this same dog to sleep on the floor later when it gets bigger. This is a non-issue 99% of the time. When that day comes, you will just create a cozy spot on the floor in your room and begin by tethering the dog in that area to teach it where its new bed is.

Graduating Steps:

a. Very young puppies may need to be in bed with you.

b. Growing puppy now gets moved to the floor, but by tethering them you are still minimizing their area. They will wake you up if they need to go potty.

c. As the puppy matures and is demonstrating good bladder control it will likely also have completed teething. Next step, give it full access to the bedroom overnight.

d. After a few months, at least 6 to 8 weeks, you might begin leaving the bedroom door open overnight. **How much of an expanded area you give at first is at your discretion.** Then continue to strategically expand the area overnight until it has access to the same areas you would like it to have when you are gone during the day.

During the Day When You are Home

Here, too, many dog owners will take gradual steps towards giving their dog more and more freedom by expanding the areas of the house that the dog has available to them as they become more trustworthy. The goal is the same: expanding the areas you want your trustworthy dog to have access to. I know it's hard but it's worth repeating: if you want a dog to be trustworthy, you have to take steps towards trusting them.

Remember that by rotating the toys you make available to your dog each day you will help them to stay interested in their own toys instead of your things.

When You Have to Be Gone For a Substantial Period of Time

A puppy/dog should again be in a controlled environment where it does not have the opportunity to get into trouble. This could be:

a. Outdoors if the environment is safe and weather is permitting.
b. Indoors in a controlled area of the house.
c. In a crate, provided crate training is a feasible environment for this dog.
   Note: Dog beds, blankets or absorbent surfaces (puppy pads) should never be left in crates if the puppy is still teething as these can be torn up and destroyed.

d. In an exercise pen, which is a valuable tool for controlling the environment.

e. Through the use of a dog gate to minimize access to other areas of the house.

At the Same Time
It's Always Time for Your Dog to Experience Being Left Home Alone ... With Free Run

The Leaving and Returning Exercise Done Right!

Dogs learn from experience. When they learn that being left home alone to freely roam the house is a normal, natural occurrence, then that's just what it is. People sometimes NEVER give the puppy the opportunity to experience being left alone until they are grown up, and then the dog freaks out at this new freedom, gets excited or frustrated, and the dog owner pays the price.

Your leaving and returning is a natural fact of life and your puppy/dog just needs to understand that. **Even with a very young puppy, it is important to start practicing this exercise early on, as soon as you get him.** Our job is to let him experience it in a way that won't frighten or frustrate him.

Based on the knowledge that **most destructive behaviors occur during the first 30 minutes after the owner walks out the door,** our goal becomes training and testing our dogs to be comfortable with being left home alone for at least 45 minutes after we first leave. When they are well behaved during the first 45 minutes after you leave, this is also a pretty clear indicator that they will also be good for several hours.

In order to stack the deck in your favor you want to:

a. Make sure your puppy/dog has been well exercised both physically and mentally and is either ready for a nap or is feeling content.

b. Make sure your puppy/dog is well fed and not hungry.

c. Make sure your puppy/dog has had ample opportunity to recently relieve itself outside.

d. Leave the dog door open, if you have one.

e. Have your departure toys available. By departure toys I'm referring to new toys or unique toys and things to chew on that are only made available at the time of your departure and during your absence.

f. Begin practicing leaving and returning.

First, get your keys, your purse, your coat, and anything you would normally get before you go somewhere and go. This means you go out the door, get in your car, and leave. The first trip you would leave for about 4 minutes and then come back home. When you come in the door you may greet your dog, but it should be <u>No</u> <u>Big</u> <u>Deal</u>. Put your stuff down, wait 5 minutes, and then leave again.

Now, depending on how you were received the first time you came home would determine how long you will be gone for your next excursion. If the puppy/dog was concerned and looking for you, I would recommend repeating the 4 minute departure time for as many times as necessary. On the other hand, if when you came home the puppy/dog was happily busy chewing on its toy and barely acknowledged your arrival, then the next trip would be for 10 minutes.

It is also a good idea to give a puppy potty breaks fairly frequently when you come home just in case the excitement has increased their the need to relieve itself.

Keep repeating this leaving and returning exercise, gradually increasing the length of time that you are gone, **for at least a half an hour ... or even an hour if you can stand it.** We want the dog to experience your leaving and returning to the degree that they are bored with the whole production. This only happens with a lot of repetition in a condensed period of time.

We can't explain to a dog that we will be back, they need to experience it.

I can't emphasize enough how important this exercise is for all dogs, of all ages and for all of the conditions mentioned in this book. You can teach your dog to be well behaved during your absence and live happily ever after.

Thunderstorm Phobia

When a dog owner shares that the dog is suffering with Thunderstorm Phobia my heart always sinks for a moment. The dismay I feel comes from knowing that there is really no strategy that will cure this fear for the dog. As an inherent condition for the dog, this means it will also be a life-long management task for the dog's owner. However, there are solutions that will bring comfort to both the dog and the owner and will minimize escape behaviors that can cause damage to the home.

Since each dog is unique, the levels of anxiety experienced during a thunderstorm can vary dramatically. A dog's experience may range from mild anxiety to an extreme phobic reaction. **What we do know is that the level of anxiety, whatever that may be, tends to increase with age due to exposure.** Once again, it is not the chronological age of the dog but rather the amount of repetition that comes with exposure that worsens the condition with age. One cruel consolation that may also occur with age is the onset of deafness. The deafness that comes with old age may bring relief from the anxiety once and for all.

It is in both the dog owner's best interest as well as the dog's to minimize the amount of stress the dog experiences at an early age. By doing this you can decrease the onset of a worsened condition that may develop with age.

Strategies that *may help* are:

a. **Talk to your veterinarian.**
    This is one time when medicating your dog early is a viable option.

b. **Consider holistic remedies for dogs.**
    There may be a holistic veterinary clinic in your area or you may also have a holistic pet supply store nearby.

c. **Discover music that your dog finds calming.**
    Even prior to a thunderstorm you may experiment to find a radio station or a particular CD that plays music that your dog finds calming. Playing this music before you go to bed could condition your dog to rest when it is being played. Playing this same music at a higher volume may bring comfort during a storm since the dog is pre-conditioned, and it may also help drown out the noises associated with a storm. It's also a good idea to leave this music playing when you're away from home if you even suspect a storm may occur.

d. **Find a place where your dog feels safer.**
    It is easier to teach your dog to go to a place that it finds comforting in the early stages of Thunderstorm Phobia. Many dog owners have shared with me that their dogs have found comfort by retreating to their bedroom closet. The closet provides the dog with comfort by: **blocking out any view of the lightning,** providing a **small space that the dog finds comforting** but also provides **freedom of movement at the same**

time. The closet most likely helps **insulate them from the noise** as well. These are all factors that you may want to take into consideration as you prepare a place where your dog feels safer.

e. **Test out garments that are designed to reduce your dog's anxiety.**

Thanks to the life of Dr. Temple Grandin, we have learned how comforting swaddling pressure can be during an anxiety attack. (If you haven't seen her movie entitled *Temple Grandin (2010)* yet, I highly recommend you do so.) In short, Dr. Temple Grandin, being autistic herself, led a life that was filled with anxiety attacks. It was as a result of her learning how to manage her own anxiety by applying a swaddling pressure from an external source that this concept developed into products for dogs.

www.ThunderShirt.com

The MarkOut Wrap®

www.MarkOut.com

It makes sense! Deaden the noise and calm the dog.

For most dogs, it is the noise that sends them into a panic. Wrapping the MarkOut® Wrap **around a panicked dog's head** can have a calming swaddling effect and soften the noise at the same time.

I discovered this method out of desperation when I was trying to help one of my clients. **This method should be reserved for dogs exhibiting a more phobic response.** For my client's phobic dog, this method brought calm to the moment and helped everyone get a good night's sleep.

Additional Steps That Can Help Deaden the Noise During a Thunderstorm:

Step 1: Use an eyedropper to put a few drops of mineral oil in both of the dog's ears. Similar to the experience you have when you have water in your ears; the mineral oil will help to deadening sound. **Step 2:** Put a couple of cotton balls in each ear to contain the mineral oil and further soften the noise.

Step 3: Wrap the MarkOut® Wrap around your dog's head to hold everything in place. The MarkOut® Wrap is made of a patented material which offers breathability. There are also Velcro strips at each end making it easy to hold the wrap in place.

Note: Once again, this method is only recommended for highly phobic dogs. You would also have to be home with your dog in order for this to work.

f. **Redirect Your Dog.**

For dogs that are only slightly anxious, you may be able to take their mind off of the storm by redirecting them to do something else they consider fun. Counter-conditioning might look like giving them their favorite chew item and basically associating the moment with something positive rather than something to be feared.

g. **Google "thunderstorm phobia in dogs."**

There are a whole host of other products such as desensitization audios or pheromones dispensers, which can be plugged into the wall to release pheromones. Pheromones can also have a calming effect on anxious dogs. In addition, there are numerous articles on the topic that I encourage you to read.

h. **BY ALL MEANS, MICROCHIP YOUR DOG.**

Most of us have seen dogs that have gotten out of their yard during a thunderstorm trying to escape the noise. **It is an uncontested fact that the dog that is wearing a collar and tags is much more**

likely to be helped by a passerby. But JUST IN CASE your dog didn't have its collar on that day, having your dog microchipped is the best protection should it escape.

Escape Behavior

Most destructive behavior that occurs during a thunderstorm is done during the dog's attempt to escape the noise and the environment it is in. Once again, having a dog door in place may reduce the likelihood that the dog would scratch up windows and doors trying to get out of the house. **This same dog may also be a great candidate for a pet containment system on the exterior fence so that once it is outside it can choose not to try to escape by means of jumping the fence.**

It Is Important to Pre-Train Dogs with Thunderstorm Phobia by Giving Them:

1. A safe place to go to inside the house.
2. Freedom of movement from inside to outside with a dog door.
3. An advanced understanding of areas of the house and yard, such as the fence, that they want to AVOID before they ever go into a panic.
4. As many of the previously listed strategies as possible to keep your dog and your home safe. It's always better to be safe than sorry.

Prevention

All dogs do not have thunderstorm phobia because this is an inherent trait that plagues a chosen few. Through very selective breeding practices, breeders can have an impact on reducing the numbers of dogs that are afflicted. In the same breath, I also want to point out that the best of breeders will always be haunted by genetic conditions that surface from time to time because they are impossible to extinguish.

I'm just saying that if I were going to purchase a puppy from a breeder, **regardless of the breed**, I would engage the breeder in a story about a dog I had once with Thunderstorm Phobia. I want to know if they ever had to go through that with any of their dogs. If they told me that the mother/father/grandmother/grandfather of the litter I'm considering suffered with it, I would politely get out of there and take my chances elsewhere with a different breeder.

I'm just saying ... that's what I'd do!!!

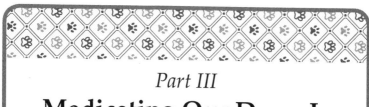

Part III
Medicating Our Dogs: Is Taking a Pill the Answer?

Could the solution be that simple? As a society we have become more and more dependent on taking prescription drugs as a solution. This trend has trickled down to the veterinary industries and the treatment of dog behavioral issues as well. It has gradually become **"the road most travelled"** by many, but does that make it right?

The drug companies certainly want us to prescribe to their solutions. Drug companies make it their business to promote drugs by advertising to the general population and to *doctors and veterinarians.* **Prescribing medication is big business.**

In 2011, I had the opportunity to attend a mini seminar given by a Veterinary Behaviorist. Across the country there are only a handful of veterinarians who are accredited as Veterinary Behaviorists. To become a Veterinary Behaviorist a person must earn the degree as a DVM, as well as specialize in behavior and earn additional certifications in this area.

The topic of this particular seminar was Pet Separation Anxiety. I knew that this particular veterinarian had a reputation for prescribing medication to most clients regarding behavioral issues. What I also learned was that this veterinarian's belief system and training led to the belief that all thinking was a result of brain chemistry. Therefore, if behavior was inappropriate, it made perfect sense to this doctor to first alter the brain chemistry with medication to modify behavior. So the seminar ended up being about why medication works in addition to behavior modification techniques.

Life is all about making choices and you are the only one that gets to choose what's right for you and your dog. The Integrated Approach to dog training acknowledges that the vast majority of behavioral issues are manageable without drugs; however, there are indeed instances when medication is necessary.

During my professional career, I have enlisted the assistance of veterinarians to prescribe medication for the following behavioral conditions:

a. Obsessive Compulsive Disorders
b. Rage Syndrome
c. Thunderstorm Phobia

Obsessive Compulsive Disorders are a wonderful example of the brain's chemistry driving the behavior. I am referring to a dog that obsesses about a particular behavior to the degree that it is damaging to its own quality of life. An example of this might be a dog that chases shadows to the degree that it cannot even go outside to eliminate like a normal dog because as soon as it gets outdoors, the obsession to chase shadows takes over. It's like a light switch goes on and nothing else matters. Another example would be the dog that absolutely has to have a toy in its mouth. This dog is so concerned about not letting go of its toy that it is actually lacking proper nutrition and losing weight because it won't let go long enough to eat a proper meal. I could go on and on with examples, but you get the idea. There is a chemical imbalance in the brain. Medication is necessary and may provide lifesaving results.

I understand that with these conditions:

a. The dog is powerless over its own behavior.
b. Behavior modification techniques will not be helpful.
c. There is nothing anyone can do to have an impact on what is causing the condition because the root of the cause is physiological.
d. Medication has proven to be the solution. The dog may actually be able to live a normal life as long as it remains on the medication.

I am all for doing what's best for a dog and its owner!!!

Rage Syndrome and Thunderstorm Phobia have nothing in common other than that the root cause in both of these conditions is also inherent and physiological.

Here again, the right medications may make all the difference in the world for the dog's quality of life.

Responsible dog owners always have a veterinarian that they entrust their dog's healthcare to. Especially when a dog is new to a family, puppies need to go in for shots and even an adult dog would normally begin with a wellness checkup. **We entrust our dog's physical wellbeing to our veterinarians.**

This does not mean that most veterinarians are also good resources for behavioral solutions. It's not uncommon for a dog owner to share concerns they may be having regarding their dog's behavior, *as a second thought*, when they are in for the dog's medical appointment. I understand the dog owners need to ask questions and seek help. I also understand that veterinarians, wanting to be helpful in every way, may want to **provide you with answers and medications** that may steer you down the wrong path.

In my opinion, responsible veterinarians:

a. Understand that veterinary practices may lose as much as 10% to 15% of their repeat clientele annually due to behavioral issues that were not dealt with effectively. Behavioral concerns that are not addressed properly are oftentimes life threatening for the dog, as this is the dog that is ultimately abandoned elsewhere.

b. Refer dog owners' behavioral concerns to a qualified dog trainer/behavior management specialist in the area. Caring veterinarians are often times an excellent referral source. They understand that they cannot take the time themselves to investigate what's really going on in each situation.

c. Understand that the dog owner's assessment of the situation may be skewed in comparison to what's actually going on. If and when the dog owner's assessment is inaccurate, then any advice or medication that the veterinarian may be tempted to provide may also be inappropriate and actually do more harm than good.

d. Do not prescribe medication for behavioral issues unless the client has first met with a qualified dog trainer/behavior management specialist. An exception to this rule would be the three behavioral conditions mentioned above:

- Obsessive Compulsive Disorders
- Rage Syndrome
- Thunderstorm Phobia

While many veterinarians specialize in certain areas, most of them are more like our own primary care physicians. Specializing in behavior management is truly a specialty.

A dog owner will almost always be best served by consulting with a qualified dog trainer/behavior management specialist first when seeking behavioral advice.

In Conclusion

Behavior Never Lies!

People can be hard to read. They may say one thing and then do another. But my rule that "Behavior Never Lies!" will not lead you astray with dogs. You can trust behavior.

The purpose of this book is to save dog's lives. Shortly after I became a dog trainer I became painfully aware of how many dogs are killed each year, largely because people do not know how to manage them.

If a child is badly behaved we don't say, "That's a bad child. Get rid of it." No, we say, "Where are that child's parents?" Someone accepts responsibility for the child's behavior and works to understand and correct it. If a dog is behaving badly, it deserves the same consideration. We do need to *understand* dog behavior in order to be able to *correct* it. The goal of this entire book is to shed light on **all** of the reasons

150

why dogs may be destructive during their owners' absence so that dog owners can understand the behaviors, and correct them.

When Behavior Is Misunderstood ... There Is No Cure!

I am sorely aware of how many dogs' lives are lost each year because people do not understand Containment Phobia and how it differs from Separation Anxiety. I actually feel a little guilty about what a difference I might have played in many of their lives if I hadn't played small for so long. This book is long overdue, but now it's done.

When I think of the large numbers of lives lost, my only peace comes from my faith that there is a life hereafter. A final gift that I would like to give you is the opportunity to download my first book, "Dogs Do Go to Heaven!" This is a true story about my first dog, the dog that actually made me a dog trainer. The day she made her transition, the day she died, she was able to communicate to me that there is a life hereafter. I have shared her story and some of my life's greatest lessons in this book. It's free to you to download when you go to **www.DestructiveDogs.com/AGiftForYou**.

I hope you will join me by sharing what you have learned with others, and *saving dogs' lives*.

Thank you!